The College Athlete's Guide to Academic Success

Tips from Peers and Profs

Bob Nathanson
Long Island University–Brooklyn Campus

Arthur Kimmel
Long Island University–Brooklyn Campus
and
St. Francis College

PEARSON

Prentice
Hall

Upper Saddle River, New Jersey
Columbus, Ohio

Library of Congress Cataloging-in-Publication Data

Nathanson, Bob.
  The college athlete's guide to academic success : tips from peers and profs / Bob Nathanson,
Arthur Kimmel.
    p. cm.
  Includes bibliographical references and index.
  ISBN 0-13-237947-3 (pbk.)
  1. College athletes—Education—United States.   2. College athletes—United States—Life skills
guides.   I. Kimmel, Arthur.   II. Title.
  LC2581.N38 2008
  378.1'98—dc22   2006027703

Vice President and Executive Publisher: Jeffery W. Johnston
Executive Editor: Sande Johnson
Development Editor: Jennifer Gessner
Editorial Assistant: Lynda Cramer
Production Editor: Alexandrina Benedicto Wolf
Production Coordination and Text Design: Thistle Hill Publishing Services, LLC
Design Coordinator: Diane C. Lorenzo
Cover Designer: Jeff Vanik
Cover Image: SuperStock
Production Manager: Pamela D. Bennett
Director of Marketing: David Gesell
Marketing Manager: Amy Judd
Marketing Coordinator: Brian Mounts

This book was set in Bookman by Integra Software Services. It was printed and bound by
R.R. Donnelley and Sons Company. The cover was printed by R.R. Donnelley and Sons Company.

Pearson Education Ltd.   Pearson Education Australia Pty. Limited
Pearson Education Singapore Pte. Ltd.   Pearson Education North Asia Ltd.
Pearson Education Canada, Ltd.   Pearson Educación de Mexico, S.A. de C.V.
Pearson Education–Japan   Pearson Education Malaysia Pte. Ltd.

10 9 8 7 6 5 4 3 2 1
ISBN-13: 978-0-13-237947-2
ISBN-10:   0-13-237947-3

Foreword

College is a grand opportunity. It is a chance to explore new worlds, some unimagined. New perspectives, new ideas, new cultures will offer themselves. If the college or university is residential, there will be new living environments. The degree and kind of change undergone by entering freshmen is rarely, if ever, duplicated in later life.

The excitement about entering college is palpable. For many, it is the beginning of adulthood, of separation from routines and persons familiar, of developing new lifestyles and making new friends. But it is also a time of increased accountability. Becoming your own master means taking responsibility for your actions.

For student-athletes, it is both easier and harder to adjust to and succeed in college. It is easier because there is an already existing framework in which you fit; there is already a network of like-minded future friends—namely, teammates—and there is already a routine for the use of your time. But it is also harder for student-athletes. Participating in sports is not the problem. Each student-athlete entering college knows how to do that, and do it well. Rather, the challenge is integrating sports into your new life. The time pressures and other challenges faced by student-athletes are more intense than for most other students. Creating a balance in your life between sports and school is essential for success but not easy to achieve.

And it is easy to fail, very easy. Most students who have a difficult time in college, including those who play sports, begin their downward spiral early in their college careers—indeed often during the first half of the first semester. It is critical that you as a new student get off to a good start if you are to succeed in college.

Success is measured, of course, not only athletically but also academically. Very few students have an opportunity to become professional athletes. For almost every student-athlete entering college, the best option for a happy and secure life depends on academic achievement. Playing sports in college is an extraordinary opportunity, but receiving your degree, gaining a basic knowledge toolkit, and learning how to learn are the real benefits of going to college.

Wouldn't it be great if instead of each entering student having to discover for himself or herself the best path toward success, there was a guidebook to show the way? Wouldn't it be useful to have easily accessible the wisdom of students who have themselves succeeded, and of faculty members who see students' struggles from an objective point of view? The good news is that now there is just such a guide.

Professors Nathanson and Kimmel have developed an invaluable guidebook for student-athletes, *The College Athlete's Guide to Academic Success: Tips from Peers and Profs*. This is not a watered-down version of the courses taken by typical first-year students. Rather it is a compilation of sage and tested advice on how to succeed in college.

The best way for student-athletes to use this book, it seems to me, is to read it in the last half of their senior year in high school or in the summer before they enter college. More important, it should be reread in part or whole during the first year. Waiting until the freshman year is underway may be too late.

College is not wholly about reading textbooks, going to lectures, and taking notes. It is an opportunity to form and solidify values, explore and establish life goals and plans, and develop habits of mind and body that take you through life. It is a time, too, to enjoy yourself. Participation in athletics contributes to these out-of-classroom experiences. But college is—lest we forget—also about reading textbooks, going to lectures, and taking exams. Indeed, college is first and foremost about learning and becoming educated! Success in college depends on academic success, not just athletic achievements. Professors Nathanson and Kimmel's guide tells how—explicitly and directly—to do both well: how to succeed academically and how to set the conditions for athletic success.

Succeeding academically, just as succeeding athletically, is hard work. Even for those with significant intelligence and natural talent, success is the result of persistence and concentration. Mistaken dead ends can be avoided. Knowing how to study, how to take advantage of what college has to offer, and how to balance sports and schoolwork are all learnable skills. *The College Athlete's Guide to Academic Success* is an excellent way to learn these skills.

The National Collegiate Athletic Association (NCAA) is an association of universities and colleges focused on sports. Its primary mission, as I have emphasized as president of the Association, is the success of those who participate in college sports, the student-athletes. "Success" is defined in terms of success both in the classroom *and* on the field of play. As far as the NCAA is concerned, a student who fails academically but is a star on the field is simply a failure. That is why the NCAA has strict rules about who is initially eligible to play in college. These rules ensure that those who attend college as athletes are prepared academically. That is also why the NCAA has strict rules about continuing eligibility to play throughout your college career. If you are performing poorly academically, you will lose your chance to play.

College can be a life-changing opportunity, one in which knowledge is gained and athletic goals achieved. By preparing well for this opportunity, students can achieve greatly and have fun doing so. Failure is no fun at all. Professors Nathanson and Kimmel have taken the mystery out of success in college by providing a most useful and readable guide.

Enjoy this guidebook and enjoy college!

Myles Brand
President, NCAA

Preface

Where We're Coming From

As professors at Long Island University in Brooklyn, New York, we've been colleagues for over 15 years. Although in different academic departments—Bob in teaching and learning and Arthur (who also teaches at St. Francis College) in sociology and social work—we got to know one another well through many years of collaboration in a precollege program that prepared students, both academically and socially, for college life. We discovered that we share similar views not only about what it takes to become a successful college student, but also about specific populations of students and the challenges they face because of their unique circumstances.

Along the way, we also realized that we both have a strong interest in one particular population of students: competitive athletes. Perhaps our interest arose because we are both sports enthusiasts, although neither of us was good enough to play at the college-varsity level. More likely, though, it's because we have a great deal of admiration and respect for those who manage successfully to face the challenges and balance both sides of the student-athlete equation. In addition, we share the same concern: Too often student-athletes enrolled in our courses and in courses taught by our colleagues don't do as well academically as we think they could and should. Although some excel, others just do so-so; yet it's clear they have the academic potential to do better. And what troubles us most is that too many student-athletes just barely manage to squeak by, and others aren't passing at all.

From our research, it became clear that of the 700,000 student-athletes who compete in college athletics each year (and over 7 million who play high school sports), far too many are not successfully meeting the challenges they face in the classroom. And we are not alone in this observation. Beginning with the 2001 publication of the landmark Report of the Knight Commission on Intercollegiate Athletics, *A Call to Action: Reconnecting College Sports and Higher Education*, significant attention has been paid to the fact that college athletes, as a group, are underperforming academically and their graduation rates are dismally low. And in spite of laudable efforts by the National Collegiate Athletic Association (NCAA), including requiring institutions to provide educational enhancement programs for their student-athletes, development of the CHAMPS/Life Skills Program, and most recently mandating the Academic Progress Rating System, which took effect during the 2005–2006 academic year, the problem persists. The bottom line is that the lack of academic success of collegiate student-athletes is a serious issue.

We wrote this book because we want to help improve the situation. On the pages that follow you'll find realistic, down-to-earth, reader-friendly observations and suggestions that are derived from our combined 56 years of college teaching experience. And you'll also find a lot more. As part of our research, we asked colleges and universities around the country to nominate their most academically successful athletes, and from that group of nominees we selected 35 recently graduated student-athletes from 16 schools. These superior athletes figured out what they had to do to succeed in their studies as well as in their sports. And in this volume they share the insights and strategies that worked for them.

Intended Audience

The College Athlete's Guide to Academic Success: Tips from Peers and Profs is written primarily for student-athletes making (or soon to be making) the transition from high school to college, for high school junior and senior athletes hoping to play a sport in college, for those already in college who are doing well academically but want to do even better, and for those student-athletes who are struggling with their academics or not working up to their potential. It is designed to help you achieve greater success in the classroom and, more importantly, to help maximize your learning so that more of it remains with you after you graduate and move on to life after college.

This book is also useful if you are a Director of Athletics, Academic Advisor for Athletes, instructor of orientation classes that include or are designed specifically for student-athletes, coach, teacher, or professor of a student-athlete, or college or university administrator or student services professional. And for parents, or other close relatives or friends of a student-athlete, it provides a variety of insights about the academic and nonacademic challenges facing student-athletes and offers a range of practical and proven ways of addressing them.

Focus of the Book

By design, this book speaks *in the voice* and *through the lens* of student-athletes, as well as from the perspective of professors who teach, advise, and evaluate them. So you can be sure that what you read on the following pages comes straight from the horse's mouth, so to speak!

In addition, knowing that a student-athlete's time is limited, we purposely designed the book to be concise, reader friendly, and usable. Each chapter introduces its essential issues and then offers practical *Tips from Peers and Profs* (our 35 contributing student-athletes and Profs. Nathanson and Kimmel), with highlighted student-athlete quotes that support the tips. There are also *Time-Out!* questions to help focus your thinking and immediately relate the issues to your own situation. And at the end of each chapter, you'll find *Questions to Think About* that encourage you to think more broadly about the key concerns just discussed.

Chapters 1 and 2 focus on the transition from high school to college and encourage athletes to think of themselves as capable students by putting the athletic skills that have worked for them to academic use. Chapter 3 sets forth a range of available resources to help ease your initial transition and address a variety of needs that may arise.

Chapters 4 and 5 address the critical areas of managing time and scheduling classes, and they provide numerous practical strategies and useful planning charts to help you manage your time, rather than let your time manage you. Chapter 6 provides questions to ask yourself and strategies to follow as you make decisions about selecting a meaningful major—that is, coming to grips with what you want to do after college and how to get there.

Chapters 7 through 10 deal with more academic areas of college life, focusing on successful in-class behaviors, establishing and maintaining positive relationships with faculty, effective and efficient study techniques, and test-taking strategies that can help you earn higher grades. We recognize that to do your best academically and athletically, you have to be at your best both physically and emotionally. Chapter 11 will help you get there, by pointing out a variety of "do's," cautioning you about the need to avoid a range of "don'ts," and providing a list of helpful resources promoting health and wellness.

Finally, just as early chapters offer ideas to help you make a successful transition from high school to college, Chapter 12 provides valuable suggestions to assist you in making a smooth transition from college to a successful and meaningful life after graduation. This chapter looks at the experiences of our 35 contributors and relates the lessons they learned as they reflect on their student-athlete days, what they took with them from their college experiences, and what they look forward to as they ponder the future.

How to Use This Book

As you can see, *The College Athlete's Guide to Academic Success: Tips from Peers and Profs* takes you full circle, moving from the transition into college, to getting the most from the experience, to transitioning away from it. We encourage you to begin at whatever point best meets your particular needs. For incoming freshmen, selected chapters or the entire book may be assigned as required reading for an Orientation to College course. Or if it's not assigned reading, you can go through it chapter by chapter. But you don't have to. For example, you may be a sophomore and realize you're having difficulty managing your time. Focusing on Chapter 4 might provide the help you need. Or you might be at the point where you're thinking about selecting a major or changing the one you've previously chosen, in which case it might be useful to go directly to Chapter 6. Or if you're questioning the value of getting a college education and wondering whether all the hard work is worth it, you might go right to the final chapter. Wherever you happen to be in your college career, even if it hasn't yet begun, we created this book for you. So we urge you to truly make it yours and make it work for you.

The College Athlete's Guide to Academic Success: Tips from Peers and Profs is not another academic survival guide. Our hope, and that of your peers, is that it will enable you to go far beyond surviving, to thriving academically on your college campus, and help you find personal fulfillment after your college days are over.

Acknowledgments

Many people provided generous support, encouragement, advice, and counsel throughout the four years that we devoted to writing this book. We are deeply grateful for their contributions. Initial thanks go to Long Island University for its sabbatical policy, which enabled Bob to plant the book's research seeds, and to Ferna Phillips of Boston College, who, in the early stages, provided access to more than 30 years of vital research. Significant appreciation goes to our 35 contributing student-athletes whose honesty, insight, enthusiasm, and timely follow-through made this book possible. We also thank the sports information directors and Academic Advisors for Athletes at the students' schools for nominating them as potential contributors.

A project like this requires early and ongoing encouragement, and it was provided by James Adams, Margaret Alaimo, Gus Alfieri, Glenn Braica, Zoe Martin del Campo, Alan Chaves, Jayne Ciarlante, Bruce Collin, Ralph Engelman, Michel Faulkner, Greg Fox, Fran Frischilla, Ron Ganulin, Michael Hittman, John Isaacs, Sam Jones, Tom Konchalski, T. J. Kostecky, Richard Lapchick, Craig Masback, Bob Rohl, Gale Stevens-Haynes, John Suarez, Larry Trachtenberg, and Betty Whitford. We thank you.

We also want to express our appreciation to all the student-athletes we've taught over the years for providing the anecdotal classroom experiences on which this book is based. You've taught us a great deal and helped us appreciate the challenges of balancing the demands of being a student and an athlete on a college campus. Particular thanks to Isaiah Cartledge, Michele Cicero, Camilla Harris, Tricia Metzger, Erin Pinchbeck, Tina Prickett, and Sonia Zapata for their honest feedback and willingness to share time management wisdom.

Sincere thanks go to Executive Editor Sande Johnson and her staff for their belief in this project and Senior Project Editor Amanda Hosey Dugan of Thistle Hill Publishing Services for her insight and professionalism. Appreciation also goes to our reviewers for their invaluable insightfulness, knowledge, and honesty: Pamela Czapla, Lock Haven University–Clearfield; Chris Helms, Virginia Tech; Jennifer Jones, Bradley University; Roy Kortmann, Long Island University; Rich Kosik, New York City Public Schools Athletic League and Reebok ABCD All America Basketball Program; Matthew Scally, Long Island University; and Alexander Wolff, *Sports Illustrated*. We are also grateful to Myles Brand and David Berst of the NCAA, who have endorsed our approach, suggestions, and strategies.

Colleagues Jeff Lambert and Barry Poris deserve a special thank you: Jeff for his technological expertise related to mass mailings and photography, and for his all-around being there for us; and Barry for his expertise and assistance with writing Chapter 11.

Finally, special appreciation and love go to our families. To Bob's parents, Phyllis and Moe, and his children, Josh and Amy, for their constant of encouragement. "So what's going on with the book? Hang in there!" To his son-in-law, Jamie Nash, for wisdom, counsel, and occasional proofreading banter; and future daughter-in-law Meghan Anderson for her interest and support. And finally, to our editor, proofreader, and super-encourager, Bob's wife, Janie, for her enormous patience and understanding when he was at the computer on beautiful days.

To Arthur's sons: Daniel, for constantly demonstrating to him how difficult, important, and valuable it is to be a true student who is athletic; and Jesse, for constantly demonstrating to him how difficult, important, and valuable it is to be an accomplished athlete who is truly studious. Their support and encouragement has been bedrock. Yes, guys, it's finally done. We can have dinner now. Also, special thanks are owed to (tae kwon do) Master Linda Lutes, whose calm, quiet strength and resolve kept Arthur centered and on course. Finally to Dr. Sonia Gray, who, through all the ups and downs, ministered selflessly to his physical, emotional, and spiritual well-being.

To these people and many more: We owe ya, big time!

Bob Nathanson
Long Island University–
Brooklyn Campus

Arthur Kimmel
Long Island University–
Brooklyn Campus and
St. Francis College

Brief Contents

Contents

CHAPTER 1

Welcome to College

People told me all through college that it would be the best four years of my life, and they couldn't have been more right.

— Patricia Metzger

Congratulations! You put in considerable time and effort to get to this point, and now you've made it—you've achieved your goal. You are, or are about to become, a student-athlete on a college or university campus. You deserve to feel great about yourself and what you've accomplished. And quite possibly, as Patricia Metzger says, you are entering what will be the best four years of your life.

At the same time, however, you may also be feeling a little nervous, maybe even intimidated by the prospect of what lies ahead. After all, being a college-level student-athlete involves experiences and challenges you've never faced before. How well will you be able to handle them?

Being a university-level student is not easy. Being an athlete is even harder.... Make the best of every moment you have with your team, in your classes and everywhere you go. College can be your best friend or worst enemy—so make the best of it!

— Jenifer Martin-Flake

As Jenifer Martin-Flake implies, the transition from high school to college is a challenge for everyone, whether playing a sport or not. All college freshmen—athletes and nonathletes alike—have much in common and must deal with many of the same issues.

In college you're far more on your own. How will you respond to the freedom and independence that college students enjoy? What will you do when there's no parent around to make sure you go to bed at a decent hour, get up to make it to class on time, or attend class at all? No one to check if you eat nutritionally or feast on junk food all day? Will you keep up with your class work or pull all-nighters and cram at the last minute? Take just the easiest "gut" courses or more rigorous ones that will better prepare you for life after college?

Starting college truly changes your world. For example, you may find that your high school friends are scattered all over the country, doing all sorts of different things. That means you'll have to make new friends. Will you be open to meeting and getting to know people from different communities, social classes, religions, and cultures who have different values, tastes, and beliefs than you? Will you value and celebrate diversity?

These are only a few of the significant decisions and adjustments all students have to make when going to college, especially when attending a school away from home. But you're not just another student. You're a student-athlete, and that means for the next four or five years you'll be facing additional pressures that most non–student-athletes don't have to deal with.

> One thing to keep in mind . . . the transition from high school can be overwhelming, but you should remember that you are not alone. Many others have felt the same way.
>
> — Jill Turner

Learning to adapt to the demands of new coaches and the expectations of new teammates are challenges in themselves. Practices are likely to be longer, harder, more frequent, and may be held at different times each day, sometimes twice a day. Competition is much tougher and the season is far longer. Physical exhaustion, mental fatigue, and scrutiny by sports-governing bodies and the media may place additional pressures on you as a student-athlete. You'll be pulled in different directions by heavy time pressures and conflicting academic and athletic schedules because of practices, training, travel, competitions, athletics-related obligations, and higher expectations for performance in your sport.

> When you first come to school as an athlete, it seems like your sport is the number-one thing to worry about and you want to make a great impression on your coaches and teammates. So you seem to spend every moment doing all you can to be successful in athletics.
>
> — Darci Pemberton Desilet

But if what Darci Desilet claims is true, then what happens to the *student* in student-athlete? After all, college is supposed to be about intellectual growth, learning, classrooms, lecture halls, libraries, laboratories, art museums, and concert halls, not to mention developing new social relationships and maturing as an adult.

To Succeed Athletically, You Have to Succeed Academically

Academically, college is very different than high school for all students. Although every student has to take certain required courses, it'll be up to you to decide when to take them. You'll probably be able to choose your classes and design your own schedule (making sure classes don't conflict with team obligations). That means, if you like to sleep late, you may have the freedom and flexibility to do just that by scheduling your first class of the day for 10 or 11 a.m. And each class won't meet every day. Some may meet only once or twice a week for two or three hours at a time. So on some days you might not have any classes at all or have long breaks between classes. What's more, some professors may not take attendance, learn your name, or know whether you show up for class or not. Sounds great, doesn't it? But is it?

Will you be able to stay focused on the material presented during a long class without a break? How will you spend the valuable free time between classes or on your days off? How will you handle the temptation to ignore that annoying alarm clock, arrive late to class, or cut class entirely? The freedom of college means you have important choices to make.

Your high school teachers probably were careful to write notes or outlines on the board. They may have repeated key points, reviewed lessons before moving on, and provided individualized attention to students who needed extra help. In college, however, that won't always be the case. You may have professors who lecture the entire semester to classes of 20, 200, or 2,000 without ever using the board or stopping to take questions from confused students. For them, if you don't understand the material, it's your problem, not theirs.

In college, you'll probably be assigned far more reading from week to week than you ever got in high school, and classes will progress at a much faster pace. Yet your professors may never check on whether you've done the reading or grade all of your work. Some may assign daily homework; others may not. But keep in mind, even though the assignments won't always be called homework, you're still expected to do them. What's more, due dates for assignments may be indicated on syllabi distributed at the first class meeting and never mentioned again. Meeting the deadlines is up to you. And professors may not accept late papers or excuse missed exams. Your papers will probably have to be typed, and spelling and grammar will count. And of course, there aren't any report cards or parent-teacher conferences in college.

When you add it all up, it's easy to see why doing well in college is tough for just about everyone. But it's likely to be even more challenging for you because, like other students with extra obligations (e.g., working or parenting), as a student-athlete you have serious demands on your time and energy. Most other students are able to study or go to the library whenever they're not in class, but you may have to be at practice, in the weight room, at team meetings, or at training or physical therapy sessions. When nonathletes are in class, you're away at games, meets, or competitions. Students who don't have additional obligations seem to be able to get by on just a few hours of sleep.

When they need to, they have time to just lie down and crash. It may also be easier for them to find those precious additional hours when there's an exam to study for or a paper due the next day. But the physical demands of your sport and the pulls it creates on your time are likely to make that more difficult for you.

Are you prepared to take on the responsibilities of being a college student, *of being a student-athlete rather than an athlete-student?* Are you ready and willing to embrace the role of student? Excel in the classroom? Or if you have entered college less academically prepared than your classmates, are you willing to do what's necessary to catch up? Are you ready to play your best game academically?

Taking Advantage of All You Have Going for You

We believe you *can* do it because many of the same personal characteristics, traits, and values that have helped you perform so well as an athlete are there for you to use in your academic pursuits. Moreover, they will serve you well when you move on to life *after* college. The key is to recognize that you have these characteristics and put them to use academically.

> One thing that a lot of people miss about being a student-athlete is the mutual compatibility with regard to performance. To me, it seems that school should actually be easier for a student-athlete because we are so well-versed in being disciplined and, just like class, each sport is goal-oriented. For example, soccer is quite complementary to school. You are constantly analyzing, looking for a weakness, being aware of the entire field, anticipating your opponents' next move. It's a lot of the same stuff that it takes to excel in class.
>
> — David Ledet

As an athlete, you have had to work well with others, learn from your mistakes and setbacks, avoid becoming easily overwhelmed, and bounce back from disappointments. Most likely you've been able to accept feedback from coaches and others and take the necessary steps to improve your performance. These are the kind of abilities that have the potential to work for you academically as well, but only if you have the drive and desire to use them.

Here are some other attributes that accomplished athletes often possess:

High energy	**Mental and physical stamina**	**Perseverance**
Commitment	**Determination**	**Desire**
Focus	**Self-confidence**	**Work ethic**
Adaptability	**Decision-making ability**	**Dedication**
Integrity	**Willingness to sacrifice**	**Anticipation**

Discipline   Leadership   Goal setting

Resilience   Ability to handle pressure   Courage

TIME-OUT!

Which of the attributes listed in the text have helped *you* excel in athletics? Jot down at least two additional positive personal attributes you possess that aren't listed. How can you apply your attributes to your academics? Do you have the desire to do so?

Whether you're attending an academically selective or less selective school, or playing a high- or lower-profile sport, the attributes that helped you excel in athletics can help you achieve more in your classes. And they can make it easier to strike the critical balance that student-athletes need to maintain—in the classroom and on the playing field. Each of these will help you strengthen your academic game—*if you make the commitment to use them.*

Developing Your Academic Game Plan

Remember, you are a student-athlete. Student comes first. . . . Make school a challenge that you want to accomplish. I like being able to say that I do track *and* get my schoolwork done. It says a lot about you when you can handle all the stuff placed on your plate.

— Angela Whyte

We wrote this book to help you "handle all the stuff placed on your plate," as Angela Whyte says. Wouldn't it be great if just having this, or any book, could make you a better student? Unfortunately, that's not going to happen. The reality is that a book can't make you a better student. Only *you* can do that. But this book can help.

Think about it this way: You didn't become an accomplished athlete just because you read a book (or a library full of them) on your sport. Tips you picked up from reading may have helped. But ultimately, how well you perform is up to you. To become a varsity athlete, you had to work, train, and put in the time to hone your skills. And although it hasn't always been fun (to say the least), you know it's been worth the time and effort.

Of course, some athletes are just more naturally talented than others. And things come easier to those lucky few. It's the same with doing well in the classroom: It comes easier to some than others. But just as those who aren't "naturals" can excel in athletics, those who aren't "naturals" can excel in academics. By applying your personal attributes to your schoolwork and by using the practical insights and tips you'll find in this book, better grades and a more rewarding college experience can be yours.

This book is designed to help you successfully manage the unique responsibilities of being a student and a competitive athlete. Think of it as your academic game plan. As college professors with years of experience teaching student-athletes and working with them to improve their academic performance, we have a good sense of what works and what doesn't, much like experienced coaches. We know what pleases us in the classroom and what gets students into trouble. We also know we don't have all the answers. So we went to the real experts for advice. We asked academically successful student-athletes at colleges and universities around the country, athletes who've figured out what it takes to succeed in their studies as well as in their sports, to share their ideas and strategies with you in a realistic and user-friendly way. You can learn more about who they are and what they've accomplished by checking out their biographical profiles at the end of the book.

On the pages that follow you'll learn strategies to help you:

- Develop and maintain a positive mind-set for a winning attitude in the classroom.

- Make the best use of campus resources.

- Manage your time efficiently.

- Set up a class schedule that works best for your needs and interests.

- Select a major that has value and plan for a satisfying career.

- Get the most out of classes and build positive relationships with fellow students, faculty, and other campus personnel.

- Study and prepare for exams effectively and efficiently and do your best on them.

- Take good care of yourself physically and emotionally.

- Make a smooth and rewarding transition to life after college.

In addition, you'll find *Time-out!* features designed to help you connect on a personal level with the things you're reading about. And at the end of each chapter, we've included several questions that ask you to think about your own situation.

This book isn't going to make you smarter than you already are—it's not designed to do that. The bottom line, however, is that it will provide you with what you need to strengthen your academic game, help you enjoy the next four or five years, and give you the tools with which to build a successful life after you graduate.

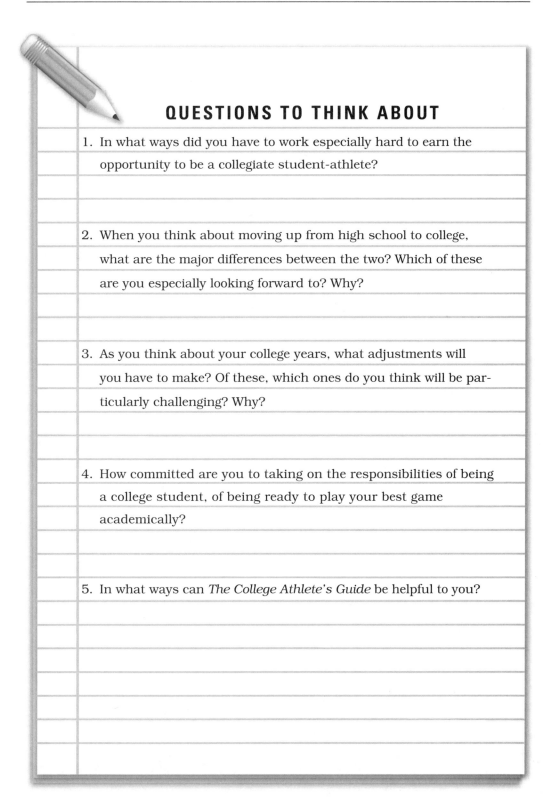

QUESTIONS TO THINK ABOUT

1. In what ways did you have to work especially hard to earn the
   opportunity to be a collegiate student-athlete?

2. When you think about moving up from high school to college,
   what are the major differences between the two? Which of these
   are you especially looking forward to? Why?

3. As you think about your college years, what adjustments will
   you have to make? Of these, which ones do you think will be particularly challenging? Why?

4. How committed are you to taking on the responsibilities of being
   a college student, of being ready to play your best game
   academically?

5. In what ways can *The College Athlete's Guide* be helpful to you?

CHAPTER 2

"I Can Do It!"

The Power of a Positive Academic Mind-Set

> You can do both—you can be a successful student as well as a successful athlete. Take advantage of this fact and put an effort into your studies as well as your game.
>
> — Jason Roberts

Many top professional and college teams, as well as world-class individual athletes, have sports psychologists on their training staffs. Ever wonder why? It's primarily because performance in competition very much depends on state of mind. You know how it works: If you're awed or intimidated by competitors or don't think you're good enough to do well against them, odds are you won't do your best. You're beaten before you even begin. But if you go into competition confidently, with a positive mind-set, you stand a far better chance of performing at the highest level. The same holds true when it comes to doing your best and performing up to your potential academically. It's critically important to maintain a positive academic mind-set.

Having a positive academic mind-set means staying true to yourself and believing in your capabilities as a student, being convinced that you want to and can *do it*, not just athletically but academically as well. It means not losing sight of the big picture, maintaining your motivation, keeping focused, and balancing your athletic, academic, and social activities today so you can enjoy the benefits of all three while you're in school and long after your college years are over.

TIME-OUT!

Why are you attending college? What would you be doing if you weren't a student? How would it pay off in the long run?

A positive academic mind-set begins with some tough questions: What do you want out of life and realistically think you can achieve? What are your long-term goals? What do you honestly see yourself doing that will bring you personal satisfaction 10, 15, or 20 years from now? How can your college education help you get there?

As if answering these questions wasn't hard enough, for you to maintain a positive academic mind-set, whether you're male or female, you may also have to confront and overcome others' perceptions of you as a "dumb jock." This is a negative, damaging stereotype.

Unfortunately, when people learn that you are a varsity athlete, they may assume that you're a typical "jock" who couldn't care less about getting a college education, even if it couldn't be further from the truth. Before they even know you, some may automatically doubt your academic abilities and question your commitment to anything but your sport and your social life. You might even come across professors who recommend that you drop their course because they say, "My class is too difficult for athletes."

Along the same lines, when friends and family know you're on a varsity team, their assumption may be that you are going to college primarily to play your sport. That's not only unfair, it's dangerous because it may be too easy for you to buy into accepting negative expectations.

Think about it: Once they know you're an athlete, what do most people ask you about? Your grade-point average (GPA) or the number of points or goals you scored? Your grade on a paper or your team's standing in the conference? The number of hours of reading you've done or the number of minutes you've played? And what determines how you're viewed by your teammates or coaches? How much time you spend in the library or how much time you spend at practice or in the weight room? When you walk into class, do your classmates and professors see you as a capable, interested, and involved student or as another "jock"? Even more importantly, how do you see yourself?

When you look in the mirror, do you see a soccer player, long-distance runner, or swimmer who happens to be enrolled in college, or do you see an English Lit major who also plays soccer, runs track, or swims on the college team? Do you think of yourself as majoring in baseball or biology? Consider the huge differences between these two images and their implications for how you grow as a person. We urge you to consider both sides of the student-athlete equation equally. You *can* excel at both!

TIME-OUT!

What's the difference between being a student-athlete and an athlete-student? Which are you? Which will be better for your long-term success? Why?

Tips from Peers and Profs

Making the Most of the Next Few Years

EXPAND YOUR HORIZONS. College is about much more than playing your sport. It offers you an opportunity that many people don't have: to gain knowledge, broaden your thinking about all kinds of issues and ideas, develop new interests, and learn more about those you already have. You can also learn a great deal from the diverse group of students and faculty who may differ from you in religious beliefs, political opinions, and personal values. You are privileged to have this opportunity. Take advantage of it—it's in front of you on campus each day in a way that you probably will never find again.

> This is a time for experience and learning. Do not make the mistake of losing perspective on your college experience—school, sport, social life!
>
> — Jason Roberts

BROADEN YOUR PLAYING FIELD. Varsity athletes tend to live together, eat together, take classes together, and study together, and as a result they may have little interaction with nonathletes. But this can dilute your college experience by isolating you from the broader educational opportunities available on campus. Try to spend some time away from athletics and athletes, getting to know and appreciate what nonathletes have to offer. For example, you might consider participating in extracurricular activities with the general student body. If you enjoy the challenge of playing chess, join the chess club; if you're into music, working at the campus radio station might be fun; if you're a psychology major, join the Psychology Club. These kinds of activities can provide personal enrichment, enhanced social and personal support, a broadened perspective on issues, and make a positive addition to your résumé when applying to graduate or professional school or for employment.

> Make an effort to meet people outside of the athletic circle. Don't let opportunities to really get to know people outside your comfort zone pass by. Everyone should experience and interact with a variety of people, and college is one of the best places to do that and to learn more about yourself from that. And listen to what people have to say, rather than just waiting for your turn to talk. . . . I have been playing sports since I was 9 and haven't explored much else since. I failed to learn that my interests lie heavily in art, drama, and music. I wonder how my life would have been different if I would have realized this earlier.
>
> — Lauren Fendrick

TIME-OUT!

Speak with three graduating teammates and discuss the nonsports opportunities that college has provided them. What opportunities are available to you? Plan how and when you will begin to take advantage of them.

Projecting a Positive Academic Image

DON'T SHORTCHANGE YOURSELF. Resist the "dumb jock" stereotype. Student-athletes deserve to be thought of—by others as well as by themselves—as intelligent, capable individuals! Getting a solid education and graduating is more important in the long run than being selected All-Conference. Define yourself as more than just an athlete. Project a positive intellectual image to those around you—friends, family, teammates, classmates, coaches, and professors—by developing and maintaining an academic persona, and they will perceive you in a far more positive way.

> Don't take it for granted that you are an athlete and settle for barely passing grades or surviving on academic probation. You wouldn't want to fail on the court, track, or field, so why do so in the classroom?
>
> — Audra Lissell

> As a student-athlete, you must balance being good at both academics and athletics. The amount of extra time you spend on your game is the same amount of time that should be spent on your studies.
>
> — Maurice Yearwood

PROUDLY SHARE YOUR ACADEMIC SUCCESSES. When friends, family, and classmates ask about your athletic accomplishments, be sure to let them also know about that good grade you got on an exam or the positive feedback you received from a professor. You take pride in your athletic performance, so why be shy about your academic personal bests?

LEAD BY EXAMPLE. Especially as a first-year student, you may feel a lot of social pressure to follow the lead of teammates and others if they encourage you to hang out in the dorm common room, get to class late or skip it altogether, or congregate in the back of the lecture hall text messaging friends or flipping through sports magazines. It takes strength and courage to resist the temptations, but those are qualities you've proven you have. So be strong and don't be intimidated by upper-class students. Set a positive example by getting to class a few minutes early, sitting up front where you're less likely to be distracted, and being ready to focus the moment class begins.

> Surround yourself with people who respect your work and your academic/athletic goals.
>
> — Ashley Ready

Maintaining Motivation and Focus

THE CRITICAL INTANGIBLE: MOTIVATION. In sports, motivation is critical. If you're not motivated to succeed, chances are you won't. It's what keeps you pushing yourself when you're physically exhausted, mentally drained, frustrated, or trying to bounce back from a poor performance. And it's essential in getting through tough times. Motivation is equally important when it comes to academics. It's the driving force behind accomplishing your academic and long-term goals. Whether you're self-motivated or motivated by outside forces, motivation is still the key to success.

> Remember that school comes first. For most of us, people will be looking at our transcripts, not our sports records.
>
> — Becky Hunnewell
>
> I have to set goals for myself. In high school, I had to get good grades so I could get into a good college. When I got to college, I had to reset my goals to keep me motivated. I decided I wanted to be a Communication Studies major because you had to have a high GPA to get in and that kept me motivated. My decision to go to grad school also motivates me to get good grades.
>
> — Katie Younglove
>
> What keeps me motivated to succeed academically is my spiritual life. There are times when you are just so tired and beat up from practice and you still have to study or write a paper. It is during these times that I pray and ask God for the strength and motivation to get through.
>
> — A. David Alston

STAY FOCUSED. Once you've decided on your goals, you need to stay focused on them. Certainly they may change as you gain experience or as your interests change, but always keep the long-term picture in mind. This may mean that you will have to work especially hard and perhaps even make some sacrifices (e.g., with free time, socializing, and recreation) to minimize distractions that could interfere with your striving to reach those goals.

> There are always going to be distractions, no matter who or where you are. There will be times when you need to study and your friends will want to go out. There are other times that there is something on TV you want to watch. It takes discipline and maturity to make yourself study when all your friends are going out, but you have to keep your values and beliefs in mind.
>
> — Jim Olds
>
> If your teammates ask you to go out with them instead of studying for your upcoming history final, say no! It takes discipline and courage. Set your priorities. Whenever I meet new recruits or incoming freshmen, I let them know they control their destiny.
>
> — Maurice Yearwood
>
> I never played video games. They can be a great way to take your mind off things, but be aware, they are addictive and can become a bad habit.
>
> — Nate Jones

TIME-OUT!

What three distractions do you anticipate having to deal with? How will you deal with them? If you're not sure of how best to deal with them, who can you turn to for advice?

When the Going Gets Tough: Managing Stress and Accepting Help

FEELING OVERWHELMED IS NORMAL. Feeling stressed is a normal reaction to new and challenging situations. Everyone experiences it at times. For example, as a college student you have the pressure of maintaining a respectable GPA, which involves handling course work, completing multiple assignments due at the same time, and preparing adequately for numerous exams. In addition, personal issues, like physical health, adaptation to campus life, social acceptance, separation from family, money problems, and relationships, at times can be highly stressful, especially for first-year students.

THE VARSITY PRESSURE COOKER. All college students face pressures. But as a student-athlete, you have additional issues like maintaining your academic eligibility and keeping your athletic scholarship or earning one. Then there are the pressures of staying on top of your game: meeting your own high performance expectations, staying healthy and injury free, and not disappointing your coaches, teammates, family, friends, and fans. If you are a star athlete, being in the limelight carries its own set of pressures and extra responsibilities. And if you don't carry star status, you might have to confront fears that you're just not "good enough" or your career is waning. Or you may harbor resentment because you feel you haven't been given the opportunity to prove yourself, or your skills haven't been appreciated or properly used. As a result, you may end up emotionally bummed out, and the additional stress can have a negative impact on your athletic performance, academic accomplishments, social life, and general well-being.

YOU _CAN_ HANDLE IT! Because you can't avoid stress (and your life would be very dull and boring without it), the key is managing it. And, believe it or not, you've already proven you know how. The fact is, you wouldn't have been able to accomplish all you have academically and athletically if you didn't know how to cope with stress successfully. In the past, when things haven't gone as well as you'd have liked, you summoned up personal characteristics like commitment, focus, self-confidence, and courage to help keep you going. You persevered and worked hard to get back to form because you believed in yourself and your abilities. You didn't let the stress hold you back. In fact, the ways you managed stressors may have even helped you achieve greater success. And they will serve you equally well throughout your college years and long after.

> Never give up. There will be days when every student-athlete is too tired or has seemingly messed up in school to the point of quitting. I have had numerous moments like that. The best thing to do is take a deep breath, analyze the situation, and rectify it in as best a way as possible.
>
> — Angela Whyte

USE COPING STRATEGIES AND TECHNIQUES. Over the years, you've employed a variety of techniques to help you cope with pressure and stress. And as you've probably learned, the best approach is probably to make sure you're as well prepared as possible for whatever you might face. But here are some other strategies that successful student-athletes have found helpful: dance or listen to music; watch a TV comedy or movie that makes you laugh; take a hot bath or relax in a whirlpool bath; meditate or practice yoga; go for a walk, run, bike ride, or swim; talk with advisors/counselors, friends, family, faculty, or others about what you're feeling; spend 10 minutes of quiet time with your eyes closed, doing nothing; talk to yourself without focusing only on the negatives or "awfulizing." And always remember to breathe. Slow, deep, diaphragm breathing is a remarkably simple, yet effective way to manage stress. The key is to identify and use whatever works for you.

> I am very competitive on and off the field. After long hours of studying and worrying about tests, I use the functions of playing my sport to manage my stress. Personally, I use soccer as my catharsis, or tension release. In the end, both academics and athletics keep me balanced.
>
> — Tim Donnelly

> The key is to know when, no matter what is going on, to take a break. Try to leave time for things that you love other than your schoolwork and your sport. Whether it be watching TV or just listening to music, you need time to yourself.
>
> — Anna (Doty) Ramirez

TIME-OUT!

What techniques do you use to manage stress? How well do they work? What other techniques might work better?

SWALLOW YOUR PRIDE AND ACCEPT HELP. Many student-athletes are reluctant to take advantage of help in addressing personal or academic issues, even when the help is easily available and confidential. They think it's a sign of weakness and it's better to simply keep quiet—suck it up and tough it out. But that attitude is often self-defeating. In reality, *everyone* needs some kind of help at one time or another. So when you even suspect you could benefit academically or emotionally from assistance, make a serious effort to put your pride and embarrassment aside, and don't be afraid to turn to the many campus resources that are designed to provide whatever help you might need. And get the help *early*. Don't wait until you're so far behind that you can't catch up.

YOU DON'T HAVE TO GO IT ALONE. Most colleges offer confidential individual counseling as well as a range of small group workshops focused on stress management and relaxation techniques. Because stress often begins with pressures in the classroom, you may want to take advantage of academic help, available from faculty and teaching fellows, your departmental advisor and Academic Advisor for Athletes, campus tutoring center, math and writing centers, residence hall advisors, as well as from fellow students and teammates (see chapter 3). Each of these will help you develop strategies to address your academic and personal difficulties, but only if you don't keep them a secret.

> You are not alone. Many others have felt the same way. Use your resources, like your teammates, coaches, and advisors to help you along the way. Never be afraid to ask for help. Also, stay on top of things from the beginning. It's a lot easier to start off well than to play catch-up the rest of the semester.
>
> —Jill Turner

 ## Remember to Enjoy Yourself: Finding a Balance

RELAX, STAY BALANCED, AND HAVE FUN. When they were freshmen and sophomores, the academically successful student-athletes who contributed to this book struggled with many of the same issues and concerns that you may face. And some of them didn't have an easy time of it. Fortunately, you can take advantage of what they learned, as early as possible in your academic career.

> Figure out what makes you happy and set your priorities. Always make time for the things that make you happiest, even when you are playing 60 games and traveling 50% of the days, and taking three tests in a week.
>
> —Ashley Ready

> Work hard on and off the court. Live a balanced life, go out and socialize, prioritize your opportunities, and college will undoubtedly be the best four years of your life. Enjoy it, but take care of business as well.
>
> —Dan Blankenship

QUESTIONS TO THINK ABOUT

1. What is motivating you to do well academically? How will those motivations help you achieve your short- and long-term goals?

2. How would you characterize your academic mind-set? Are academics your number-one priority? What are some examples of this? Are you comfortable with who you are as a student?

3. Have you ever experienced others perceiving you as a "dumb jock"? If so, in what ways? How did this make you feel? Is there anything you might have inadvertently done that contributed to this perception?

4. What steps have you taken, either in high school or in college, to ensure that you put your best foot forward as a student?

5. What academic pressures do you feel or anticipate feeling in the future? How will you address them so they don't get the best of you?

CHAPTER 3

Making the Most of Campus Resources

You will get out of college whatever you put into it. Anything you want to figure out, find, look for, learn about, do, etc., you are surrounded by amazing resources to do it. It's a once in a lifetime opportunity.

— Lauren Fendrick

O nce they arrive on campus, all college students—athletes and nonathletes alike—have to deal with an enormous number of issues they've probably never faced before. So it's no surprise that as a new student you will most likely have a lot of questions: where to get help with selecting courses, finding the best professors, getting registered, buying books, and paying your bills. How do you get your ID card, your computer hooked up, access to the library, find your classrooms? And that's just the beginning. After you've been on campus for a while, new and sometimes more complicated questions and issues often arise. How do you handle a personal problem or health concern, choose a major, find a specific book or journal article in the library, or line up a job for the summer?

At one time or another, everyone needs some kind of help. And that's especially true for college students. It's nothing to be embarrassed about. In fact, your tuition, room and board expenses, and student fees pay for a lot more than coaches' and professors' salaries and the cost of your dorm and meals. They also go to pay for a wide variety of valuable campus services that are available to help you succeed and enjoy school—not just athletically, but academically, vocationally, socially, and emotionally as well. Taking advantage of these beneficial services, though, is up to you. The key is recognizing *what you need*, knowing *where to find it*, and then getting it *without delay*.

In chapter 2, you read about the importance of accepting help and how "you don't have to go it alone." It's worth repeating. Many student-athletes are reluctant to ask for help or take advantage of it when it's available. Some think it's a sign of weakness or that they need to handle everything on their own. Whatever the reason, when a difficulty arises they often keep it to themselves and try to tough it out. But just as you've turned to coaches or trainers over the years for help in improving your skills or addressing an area of weakness, you'll find it far easier to manage college life if you take advantage of the many campus resources that are available. And the earlier you do it, the better. Don't wait until you find yourself in a hole that's so deep you won't be able to climb out. You need to be proactive rather than reactive.

What follows are typical needs that come up for students throughout their college years, and the resources that are available on most college campuses, usually free of charge, to address those needs. Make sure you know where on campus the resources are located and what hours they're available, and ask your Academic Advisor for Athletes and upperclassmen for the names of especially helpful staff in each office.

Tips from Peers and Profs

Getting Started: Admissions, Orientation, Advisement, Registration

IT BEGINS WITH ADMISSIONS. One campus resource with which every college student has had contact is the Office of Admissions. The staff in this office are there to answer applicants' questions, move their applications along, and help them navigate successfully through the admissions process. With their assistance you were able to do everything necessary and were admitted.

ORIENTATION AS A STUDENT. In competition, the kind of start you get can have a major impact on how well you do in an event. The same is true when it comes to college: It's important to jump off to the best possible start. Most colleges recognize this and require all incoming students to participate in one or more orientation programs. A general orientation, which may run for one or more days before classes begin or early in the semester, or as a semester-long course, gives students an overview of the college and its facilities, academic programs, services, policies, and procedures. It might also provide information and advice about registering for classes, obtaining your campus ID and other necessary permits, clearing your bill, getting a college e-mail address, and using the library and other campus facilities.

ORIENTATION AS AN ATHLETE. At many colleges, the Department of Athletics offers its own orientation program for student-athletes, either as an alternative or in addition to the general orientation. It will go beyond the information presented in the general orientation to inform you about policies and procedures concerning your responsibilities as a student-athlete. The intent is to ensure that your actions on and off the field are in compliance with the National Collegiate Athletic Association (NCAA) (or other governing body), your conference, institution, and team rules and regulations. You'll also be introduced to a number of individuals available to help you academically, athletically, and personally. But even though you are a student-athlete, it's not a good idea to rely solely on the resources offered by the Athletics Department. Make sure you also take advantage of the resources available to the general student body.

TIME-OUT!

As a student, what are issues you think you might need help with? As an athlete?

ORIENTATIONS MAY BE FUN, BUT TAKE THEM SERIOUSLY. Orientation sessions are designed to provide you with essential information and assistance that will help you get off to the best possible start and will be useful throughout your college career. So treat them seriously and pay attention to what goes on. At each session, be prepared to take notes, and be sure to read and save all materials that are distributed.

WHAT'S AN ACADEMIC ADVISOR? At most colleges, new students are assigned an academic advisor, and usually a faculty advisor or academic counselor in their major department once they've chosen a major. As a student-athlete, it is likely that you will also be assigned an Academic Advisor for Athletes, who will have a special appreciation of the overlapping demands of your academic and athletic responsibilities, as well as expertise in developing strategies for managing the two. Your advisor(s) will help you use the college catalog and schedule of classes, assist with selecting a tentative major, discuss required and elective courses, and help you with dropping or adding courses and scheduling classes that don't conflict with your athletic responsibilities. They might also give you a heads-up on which faculty to take classes with or to avoid. So make sure you work closely with your academic advisor(s), and ask them about priority or early registration that may be available for student-athletes on your campus.

ADVISORS CAN PROVIDE ALL SORTS OF ASSISTANCE. You can turn to your advisors for help in a variety of areas. For example, if you run into academic difficulty, you can ask them for suggestions about what you can do to resolve the problem. They'll have ideas about where you might go to find tutoring or suggest strategies on how best to discuss the situation with your professor. Of course, the key is to discuss the matter with your advisors as early as possible, before you fall too far behind.

BUILD AND MAINTAIN GOOD RELATIONSHIPS WITH ADVISORS. Make sure your advisors get to know you personally and are aware of your interests and your needs. Even if your campus has an e-mail advisement system, it's better to schedule face-to-face meetings at the appropriate times each semester. Ask for your advisors' opinions, but don't simply rely on what they suggest. Prepare thoroughly for meetings, consult the college catalog and schedule of classes, make a list of questions, be open to suggestions, and, most important of all, be sure to do your own thinking. After all, it's your life and you're the one who has to be in control of it (see chapter 5 for a discussion of this important point).

KEEP FILES OF ALL IMPORTANT COMMUNICATIONS. Record keeping is critical. You'll be receiving a lot of college mail, both in hard copy and e-mail formats: proof of registration for classes, grade reports and transcripts, bills, receipts for payments made, and letters from advisors and professors, for example. Too many students take a quick glance at the mail and either toss it in the trash or into a desk drawer, delete it, or, even worse, they don't look at it at all. But the mail is usually important, or the school wouldn't spend the time and money sending it to you. So set up a record-keeping system. Carefully file and keep hard copies of all materials that you might need at a later date. And don't forget to read both your snail mail and e-mail and to respond to all that require a response.

TIME-OUT!

Purchase an inexpensive file holder or find an appropriate-size plastic or cardboard box and set up your own filing system. What categories do you think you'll need?

OFFICE OF THE REGISTRAR. The registrar's office publishes the schedule of classes and processes your registration for classes each semester. You declare or change your major and add or drop classes with this office. The registrar maintains students' academic records, gathers all course grades, and computes your GPA. In addition, the registrar determines whether or not you have taken all required core classes, as well as those required for your major, and awards your degree. This office also processes transfer credits from other colleges and provides official transcripts needed for graduate and professional school applications, employment, and transferring to another school. But keeping track of your grades and progress toward your degree is ultimately your responsibility. So at the end of each semester, carefully check your transcript online or in hard copy form, and keep a copy of it in your files.

Dealing with Dollars and Sense: Financial Aid, Bursar, Bookstore

WHO'S PAYING THE BILLS? Before college, most students don't have to worry about how to meet the costs of tuition, fees, textbooks and supplies, or room and board. But as a college student, you'll probably have to take on more of the financial responsibility for your education. After all, your school wants to know how you are going to manage the costs of attendance. And whether you are attending a publicly funded or private college, there are considerable expenses. Even if you have a full scholarship, the Financial Aid Office will be involved in making sure you are able to meet those costs. This is called "clearing your bill," which must be done before the start of each semester so you can attend class. Note that clearing your bill does not mean the bill has been paid, but only that arrangements have been made to pay it. If there are gaps in your financial aid, financial aid counselors are available to let you know what scholarships, grants, loans, and other forms of aid are available and how to apply for them.

A FEW WORDS OF CAUTION. Many financial aid programs have strict application deadline dates. Be sure to follow them. Also, be very careful about applying for loans and credit cards. Scholarships and grants don't have to be paid back. But loans and credit card debt do—and with interest, often lots of it, especially with easy-to-get credit cards. Credit card debt has financially ruined many students. Although the offers may be inviting, and you may be able to get your hands on a lot of money quite easily, do so only as a last resort and only to meet educational expenses. Don't fall into the trap of using so-called easy money to buy large screen TVs, high-end music systems, expensive clothing, or lavish gifts for friends and family. If you do, you'll end up paying for them for a long, long time, and with a frightening amount of interest.

WHAT'S A BURSAR? The Bursar or Cashier's Office handles all matters related to paying and clearing your bill. The staff works closely with the Financial Aid Office. If you are receiving an athletic scholarship, be sure to present the necessary paperwork from the Department of Athletics to the Bursar's Office and stay in touch with them until your bill is cleared. This office may also be helpful by offering check-cashing services for students with a valid campus ID.

YOU'LL NEED TO BUY TEXTBOOKS. In high school, your textbooks were probably handed to you by your teachers and you returned them at the end of the term. So you didn't have to give any thought to how much they cost. In college, though, the average cost of required textbooks and supplies can run to about $1,000 or more each academic year. And it's *very wise* to buy them. That's why it's a good idea to comparison shop. All colleges have a campus bookstore, but there may also be competing bookstores in town that sell required texts and materials at a better price. To save money, it's a good idea to check them out. Also, take a look at online discount book sites where prices will be lower, although you might have to pay shipping costs that could cut into any savings. Remember, too, that books purchased online take time to be delivered. So if you need a book immediately, buying it online may be a bad idea (for other ways to possibly save on textbooks, see chapter 9). The campus bookstore also stocks all the basics such as backpacks, pocket calendars and organizers, calculators, notebooks, and pens. Here again, though, comparison shopping at discount office supply stores could mean savings.

Moving Beyond College: Career Services, Community Service

WHAT IF YOU CAN'T TURN PRO? Perhaps you've dreamed of getting out of school and signing a long-term multimillion dollar pro contract, along with all sorts of lucrative promotional deals for products. We hope your dream comes true. Unfortunately, the chances of that actually happening are minimal. Only about 1% of college athletes go on to compete professionally, and of those who do, most have pro careers that last less than 5 years. So you need to consider other options for what you might like to do after you graduate. The courses you take are linked to what you decide to major in, and what you major in can affect the career opportunities that become available to you. But more and more students are entering college without a clear sense of what they want to do with their futures. That's absolutely fine. Because whether or not you know what you want to major in or have a clear vocational goal, a variety of career planning and job placement services are available through the Career Services Office on campus. These include interest and aptitude assessment, individualized career counseling, job search preparation, résumé development, employment fairs and on-campus interviews, as well as summer employment assistance, internships, and networking with alumni.

> Be mature enough to realize that when college is over, being a professional athlete is not a viable option for most of us.
>
> — Seth Neumuller

> I wish I had put more time and energy into figuring out what I wanted to do after undergraduate school. I regret not taking full advantage of career-seeking and career-furthering opportunities at school to set up contacts that would have put me on a path consistent with my aspirations.
>
> — Lauren Fendrick

VISIT CAREER SERVICES EARLY AND OFTEN. Too many students, especially athletes who have dreams of competing professionally, wait until their last semester to take advantage of career services. They don't concern themselves with serious thinking about vocational possibilities. That's not wise. The smartest thing to do is begin your career planning early and to be open to exploring a variety of career and professional options. Through the Career Services Office you may learn that you have talents, strengths, and interests you never realized you had. And don't kid yourself: Even if you are fortunate enough to turn pro, because your career as a professional athlete won't last forever, you need to be prepared with a viable postathletic career (detailed information and suggestions about how are in chapter 5).

The Career Center here at Rice has been invaluable by helping me to organize and proofread my résumé, by creating and publicizing opportunities for meeting employers at on-campus job fairs, and by preparing me for interviews. The Career Center is where to go for help when trying to answer the question, "What careers are available to me if I decide to be a _____ major?"

— Seth Neumuller

TIME-OUT!

Visit your campus Career Center and speak with a counselor. What is the counselor's name, e-mail address, and phone number? What services are available that you might want to take advantage of?

GIVING BACK. Many colleges and athletics departments require or encourage students to become involved with community service (e.g., tutoring in local schools, visiting hospitalized children, or assisting at area soup kitchens). These unpaid activities offer students a way to contribute meaningfully to their communities and build civic-minded leadership qualities. In addition, these experiences can spark interest in a particular major, provide access to professionals and alumni in a variety of fields, and may open doors to summer and full-time employment. Information about these worthwhile opportunities may be available at your college's Service Learning or Community Service Center, or it may be handled directly through the Department of Athletics.

Finding Help with Academics: Information Technology Library, Learning Center

THE COMPUTER CENTER. In college, you'll need to know how to do more with a computer than play games, instant-message friends, and download music and movies. Because the use of information technology (IT) is increasing so rapidly, advanced computer literacy is a requirement! Students are not only expected to be proficient at word processing, but many faculty members require that you be knowledgeable in the use of presentation software, spreadsheets, course management systems, online library resources, and a range of other technologies to support online discussion groups, note distribution, and other purposes. Whether you own your own equipment and are computer savvy or not, the campus IT Center or Academic Computer Center offers a wealth of services and assistance. It typically provides a number of computer labs, stations, and printers throughout the campus, help desks to troubleshoot problems you may have, and training for everyone from beginners to more sophisticated users. Here you can also get advice on purchasing a system that is most compatible with your campus or academic discipline (some are more Mac friendly; others favor PCs). IT may even have arrangements with vendors that enable you to purchase computer systems and software at significantly reduced prices.

LIBRARIES DO MORE THAN HOUSE BOOKS. All schools have at least one college library that is open from early in the morning until late at night and provides an extensive array of resources and services. Throughout your college years you'll be expected to use the library to find books and journal articles and to search through online databases of information. Libraries may seem huge and overwhelming, but they actually have become extremely user friendly. So friendly, in fact, that many of their collections and resources (e.g., catalogs, databases, reserved readings, full-text journal articles, and streaming media) can be accessed online from the comfort of your dorm room or apartment, 24 hours a day. At the library itself, you'll find librarians to provide you with suggestions and assistance in locating whatever research materials you might need. But don't expect them to do your library research or write your term papers for you. To help you become familiar with your campus library, there's probably a library orientation offered. There you'll learn how to use the various online information catalogs and the most effective search strategies for researching specific topics. This will help you become information literate, a skill that will stay with you for the rest of your life.

> Just about every time I went to the library I would ask the people at the reference desk to help me out. The majority of people were willing and even wanted to help you out. All you needed to do was ask.
>
> — Jon Larranaga

LIBRARIES ARE GOOD PLACES TO STUDY. Another way the library can be a resource is by offering a variety of really good study spots from early in the morning until late at night. And during exam periods, some are open 24 hours. Whether you prefer an individual carrel or cubicle, a large study table, a comfortable couch, or an area for group work, the library will have it, along with copy machines, water fountains, and some of the cleanest rest rooms on campus. Look around for a study spot where you're comfortable (but not too comfortable). It should be quiet, have adequate lighting and ventilation, and be free of distractions.

> Using the school library as a place to study has been the key to my success. I often use it as a place to escape commotion when studying for long periods of time or a place to sneak in a quick review prior to a test.
>
> — Tim Donnelly

TIME-OUT!

Check out the campus library and locate a spot that feels right for reading, writing papers, and general studying. Beginning this week, try using it.

IS A COURSE ESPECIALLY CHALLENGING? At some point virtually every college student struggles with an especially difficult class. That's why most colleges have academic specialists and tutors available. You'll generally find them through the campus Learning Center, Academic Reinforcement Center, Tutoring Center, or similarly named resource. Discuss your difficulties with your professor and academic advisor as soon as you sense there might be a problem. He or she may suggest specific steps you can take to get a better handle on course material or recommend that you seek the assistance of an academic support service, such as individualized weekly peer tutoring, or perhaps drop-in tutoring as needed. The center may also offer academic enhancement workshops on topics such as study skills, time management, test anxiety, note-taking skills, and speed reading. And don't overlook the help you can get from classmates and teammates who are doing well in the courses that are giving you problems. Their strategies might be beneficial as well.

> Every college has tutoring available, but you must seek the help in order to receive it. Don't be overly proud and try to handle it all on your own. Ask your teammates, your coaches, your friends, and your administrators for help when you need it. They are resources for you—utilize their services.
>
> — Patricia Metzger

Addressing More Personal Issues: Other Needs and Interests

HAVE A PRESSING PERSONAL ISSUE? Although you'll have the emotional support of coaches, faculty, teammates, and friends, at times serious personal concerns are better addressed by a trained and experienced psychologist, psychiatrist, or social worker. Through the Counseling Center, which may be set up as a free-standing office or within the campus Health Services or Wellness Center, your college probably offers free or low-cost individualized, confidential personal counseling. The Counseling Center may also offer small-group workshops that focus on issues frequently faced by college students. These may include stress management, relationship problems, family issues, substance abuse, sexual orientation, religious and cultural differences, and motivational difficulties. You've heard it before: You don't have to go it alone. Help is available, but it won't go looking for you. You have to recognize your needs and make them known (see chapter 11).

A MENTOR CAN MAKE A DIFFERENCE. Although some schools have a formalized alumni or peer mentoring program, relationships with mentors are most often forged informally as students look to adult or older peer role models for guidance and support. Coaches, older teammates, graduate assistants, professors, or campus-based counselors typically serve as one-to-one resources for students beyond the role for which they are paid to serve on campus. These individualized relationships evolve naturally because each of the participants values the other, not solely as a student or professional, but as a person who is admired, trusted, and valued and whose support can make a huge difference.

> Some of the best relationships you form throughout your college years are with those who have been where you are now, like professors or staff members. Your best friend can't always tell you what classes to take or how to plan your future. There's nothing better than having a person you can go to not only to discuss your academic future, but the events in your life as well. That's where having a mentor comes in. Having a person to look up to is critical, especially for an athlete.
>
> — Audra Lissell

EVERYONE NEEDS TO KICK BACK SOMETIMES. At times, all students need to relax and do something just for fun. The Student Union or Student Activities Center offers a range of activities, from video games and Ping-Pong to discussion groups, clubs, and social action projects on just about anything that might be of interest to students. These provide an excellent opportunity away from the classroom and from athletic practice and competition, for you to meet new people, make new friends, share common interests and concerns, and develop new ones. You can usually also grab a drink or a bite to eat (stay away from the candy machines!), pick up a newspaper or magazine, or even check out the numerous bulletin boards for ideas on what to do with an upcoming weekend.

NOT FEELING WELL? As a student-athlete, you have access to a range of health-care providers, including physicians, trainers, and physical therapists. Don't hesitate to speak with them about your individual needs. In addition, you also can take advantage of your school's Health Services or Wellness Center. The center is usually staffed by nurses and part- or full-time physicians who specialize in working with college-age students. Most college health programs also offer a range of informational services and programs focused on such topics as human sexuality, prevention of contagious diseases, and substance abuse awareness and prevention. Whether you have a cold, sore throat, or something more severe, it's important to know the center's location, the hours it's open, and the cost of services. Students may be treated free of charge or for a reduced fee. But it's likely that you will have a medical insurance plan, either from home or issued through the college, that will work hand in hand with the Health Center to pay for most medical expenses. To be on the safe side, though, it's best to be certain what your obligations will be.

ISSUES WITH A ROOMMATE OR A LUMPY MATTRESS? The Office of Residence Life or Student Housing maintains a staff of trained peer counselors or resident advisors (RAs) along with a professional administrative staff to provide for the well-being of students living on campus. The office assigns rooms and roommates, oversees meal plans, coordinates a range of activities, and addresses a variety of personal and interpersonal issues faced by students living away from home and family.

SUPPORT FOR SPECIAL EDUCATIONAL NEEDS IS AVAILABLE. Many colleges provide a range of support services for students with physical, emotional, or learning disabilities whose special needs may pose a particular challenge for them on campus. For example, a student with a documented learning disability can turn to the Disabled Student Services Office for help in arranging individualized study skills assistance, textbooks on tape, and extended time for taking exams.

LOOKING FOR OTHERS WHO SHARE YOUR INTERESTS? The Office of Multicultural Affairs, Women's Center, International Students' Office, Office of Minority Student Services, and Center for Nontraditional Students are among the kinds of resources provided for members of the college community with specific interests. If you're looking to spend time with others who share your religious affiliation, you can turn to campus organizations such as the Newman Club, Hillel, or the Muslim Students League. Many campuses also have an interdenominational chapel and campus-based ministry, offering religious services, space for meditation and reflection, and pastoral counseling. If there isn't already an organization that reflects your interests or affiliations, you may want to consider starting one.

BE PREPARED FOR AN EMERGENCY. Ideally, you'll never need to use them, but it's a good idea to keep the phone number of your college's department of security or campus safety department readily available.

HELP WITH CHILD CARE. If you are the parent of a preschooler, your college might provide an on-campus day-care center that offers low-cost child care and educational services on a part-time or full day basis so that you can attend classes and practices with a clear mind knowing your child is well cared for.

WHEN YOU DON'T KNOW WHERE TO TURN. The Offices of the Dean of Students and Vice President of Student Affairs oversee the nonacademic well-being of the student body. The Offices of the Academic Dean and Dean of the College are responsible for all academic matters related to your education. It is unlikely that you'll have to see the deans personally, because their office staff will be able to direct you to the campus resources that most appropriately address your specific concerns. But if you feel the need, don't hesitate to ask to see the dean personally.

JUST ABOUT ANYTHING YOU MIGHT NEED IS AVAILABLE. Check out campus bulletin boards, posters and flyers taped to walls, trees, and light poles, campus and community e-mail postings, school and community newspapers, local radio and TV programs, tables set up around campus and leaflets other students distribute, religious groups, and community meetings. The list goes on and on. Keep your eyes and ears open to everyone and everything that goes on around campus. You'll find out about an amazing range of resources, along with movies, plays, concerts, exhibits, lectures, and a whole lot more.

TIME-OUT!

Of those discussed, which five campus resources do you think that, at some point, you'll need to use? Where on campus are they located? What hours are they available? Do you need an appointment or can you just drop in?

Important Resources

Keep this information readily available and up-to-date

NCAA: (371) 917-6222

Your College's Athletic Conference: _____

Web address: _____   **Phone number:** _____

	Name	Phone number	E-mail

**Academic Advisor
for Athletes:** _____

Faculty Advisor: _____

Head Coach: _____

Assistant Coach: _____

Assistant Coach: _____

Assistant Coach: _____

**Compliance
Coordinator:** _____

Trainer: _____

Health Services: _____

Academic Dean: _____

Dean of Students: _____

Campus Security: _____

**Computer Center
Help Desk:** _____

Tutoring Center: _____

Library: _____

Financial Aid: _____

**Residence Life/RA
Floor Counselor:** _____

Additional Resources

Title	Name	Phone number	E-mail

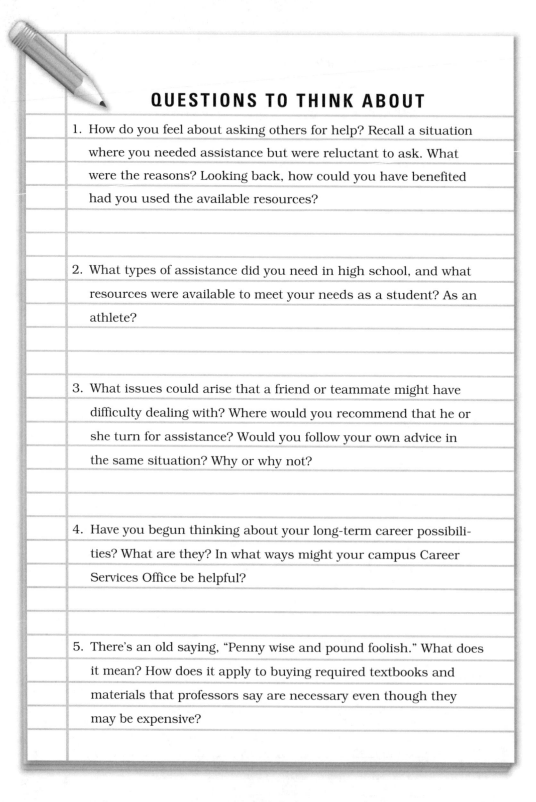

QUESTIONS TO THINK ABOUT

1. How do you feel about asking others for help? Recall a situation where you needed assistance but were reluctant to ask. What were the reasons? Looking back, how could you have benefited had you used the available resources?

2. What types of assistance did you need in high school, and what resources were available to meet your needs as a student? As an athlete?

3. What issues could arise that a friend or teammate might have difficulty dealing with? Where would you recommend that he or she turn for assistance? Would you follow your own advice in the same situation? Why or why not?

4. Have you begun thinking about your long-term career possibilities? What are they? In what ways might your campus Career Services Office be helpful?

5. There's an old saying, "Penny wise and pound foolish." What does it mean? How does it apply to buying required textbooks and materials that professors say are necessary even though they may be expensive?

CHAPTER 4

Finding the Time to Succeed

[Time management] is the most difficult part of being a student-athlete.

— Becky Hunnewell

High school's over, and you're ready to enjoy all the free time and flexibility that college students supposedly have. Sure, going to college means you may be able to set your own schedule. If you like to sleep late, you might be able to schedule your first class for 10 or 11 a.m. And some days you might not have any classes at all. It sounds like heaven, too good to be true. But unfortunately, like most things that sound too good to be true, it is. In fact, for student-athletes, time is a very precious commodity.

In spite of what you might have expected, there are tremendous time pressures on *all* college students. In fact, talk to just about any college students and they will tell you that being able to manage time and handle all the academic and social demands of college life is a major challenge.

But you're not just any student. You're a student-athlete. That means you have to deal with all the time-consuming issues that nonathletes do, and many, many more: practices, conditioning, training and weight room sessions, team meetings, morning runs, physical therapy, media interviews, film sessions, mandatory study hall, pep talks (or chewing-outs) from coaches, and community service or booster obligations. And this list doesn't even include games, meets, competitions, and road trips that can take you away from campus for 3 or 4 days at a time. If it sounds like student-athletes are under a lot of pressure, it ought to. Because, as Becky Hunnewell indicates, you are! There's no doubt about it: Playing a college sport places a great deal of additional stress on your time, energy, and focus. You have far more on your plate than most nonathletes.

Student-athletes are pulled in many directions all at once. It may feel as if you're always running, always playing catch-up, like you're on a treadmill that just won't stop. Sure, the NCAA limits team-related hours to 20 hours a week during your season. But with all the so-called voluntary activities, it may seem like being on a team is a full-time job. And if you're on scholarship, you might feel like you're working for the coach, always on call. So before you know it, you may be getting too little sleep, skipping meals, falling behind in assigned readings—cutting corners all over the place. The pressure might seem impossible, and even though you love the idea of being on the team, you could feel ready to give up. Or because you've lost sight of what's best for you in the long run, you might be willing to accept less than the best from yourself academically.

But wait! As overwhelming as it might sound, you *can* manage life as a student-athlete in ways that will allow you to succeed at both your sport and in your studies. *It is possible.* In fact, many student-athletes who are no smarter or better prepared for college than you are able to excel both academically and athletically. And if they can do it, so can you!

> The biggest key to your success will be managing your time. At some points, you may feel overwhelmed, but generally you will have time to do what needs to get done. Juggling academic and team obligations is hard but not impossible to do.
>
> — Jim Olds

Tips from Peers and Profs

 ### Time Management Is About You and Your Needs

YOU GET ONLY 24 HOURS. It all begins by accepting a simple fact: There are only 24 hours in a day. And because of the demands being a varsity athlete places on your body, you probably need to spend at least 8 of them sleeping, especially during your team's season. Then there's the time you spend showering, getting dressed, eating, doing laundry, and the like. So you may be left with, at most, 14 or so hours a day to fit in everything else you have to do: attending class, studying, writing papers, getting to mandatory study halls, going to practice, hitting the weight room, and, for some, working part time—not to mention playing in games or performing at meets and competitions. And let's not forget about a social life. Everyone needs one of those!

KNOW YOURSELF. Learn your own capabilities and limits. Remember that every person is different. What works for your teammates or other students may not work for you. So avoid falling into the trap of paying too much attention to what others do or when they do it. Get to know yourself and what works and doesn't work for *you.* Are you more awake and alert early in the morning or late at night? After a meal or after a shower? Plan your time to account for what is best for you. Schedule longer study sessions for times when you are most alert and able to maintain your focus. But keep in mind that some people study most effectively in longer, extended, uninterrupted blocks of time. Others do better using shorter blocks with scheduled breaks. Experiment and find the schedule that works for you. Then plan your time to make the best use of your 24 hours.

> Often, after 6 a.m. workouts, I'd come back to my room, shower, have breakfast, and then do a little work before class. This works because I know I have the most energy at the beginning of the day.
>
> — Johanna DiChiara-Drab

It All Starts with Planning

PLAN AHEAD. Although it's important to plan for today and tomorrow, that's not enough. Always try to plan as far ahead as possible.

> Use your time wisely. The more you can get ahead in your classes, the better. Figure out some set blocks of time that work for you (traveling/airports are awesome for this). Find a quiet place, turn off your cell phone, don't e-mail, and just get it done. If you buckle down for short periods of time (like between all of your practice times and lifting), you will not have to spend your whole weekend studying.
>
> — Darci Pemberton Desilet

USE A PLANNER. A powerful personal digital assistant (PDA) can be a useful tool, but the truth is that planners don't have to be expensive or sophisticated. In fact, for daily planning, a 3 by 5 index card works well for a simple to do list. Your school's bookstore carries pocket organizers, erasable boards, desk planners, or whatever else you are comfortable using. You might even consider purchasing two planners, a larger one for your room and a more compact one to carry with you. If you do decide to go with two planners, be sure to include all information in both. And of course, no matter what you choose, as with anything new, it may take a short while to get used to using it.

> Organization is the key. I keep a planner that has a monthly overview but allows room to write in individual days. On each month, I write out game dates and other major events. On each day in the weekly layout, I use pencil (or one color of erasable ink) to write down exams and homework due dates, use another color ink for team activities, and use a third color to jot down things that I want to get done that night. This allows me to have an overview of how busy my month will be and how busy each week will be. These features allow me to figure out how much time I need to devote to both academics and athletics.
>
> — Brandi Cross

PLAN TO INCLUDE EVERYTHING. Of course, unforeseen things come up from time to time, but they are far less of a problem to manage if everything else has been planned for. First, create a monthly (Figure 4.1), weekly (Figure 4.2), and daily (Figure 4.3) chart of your standing obligations, your must-do commitments. These would include class hours, athletic obligations (games, meets, practices, etc.), exams, due dates of reading assignments for all your classes, course paper deadlines, travel to athletic events, school vacations, family obligations, and religious commitments. Then add on your less formal to do's, where you have more flexibility with scheduling. These might include going out on dates, meeting friends for dinner or a movie, getting a haircut, doing your laundry, calling friends or family, and similar activities. You'll end up with a picture that keeps you briefed on what's going to be happening and when. It also alerts you, in advance, to "crunch" times when demands will be greatest. It's also a good idea to keep lists of quick to do's, like stopping at the ATM or picking up a container of juice.

> Student-athletes need to be the most organized students on campus. In order to balance a practice schedule, games, road trips, study hall hours, advisory meetings, class schedule, and tests, you must have a way to get your obligations taken care of without losing your sanity. My schedule, posted in my Day Planner, kept me on top of my responsibilities and allowed me to balance my priorities with my extracurricular desires.
>
> — Ashley Ready

TIME-OUT!

Using the blank planning charts provided at the end of this chapter, lay out your schedule for the coming week and month. Also, on an index card, write down exactly what tomorrow will look like. How manageable do you think these schedules will be for you?

PLAN FOR THE UNPLANNED. Be aware that things often take more time than you think they will. Meetings sometimes run long, professors may be late for your appointment with them, traffic may slow you down, and so on. So try to be as accurate as possible when estimating how long things will take, but always allow extra "just-in-case" time in your planning. As one coach often advises his athletes, "Life is 10% what happens to you and 90% how you plan for and deal with it."

GET A SECOND OPINION. As a new student it may be difficult to estimate accurately how long things will take. Why not have your Academic Advisor for Athletes or an upperclass teammate take a look at your schedule and make suggestions?

Figure 4.1 Tina's Monthly Schedule

NAME OF MONTH: April

Thursday	Friday	Saturday	Sunday	Monday	Tuesday	Wednesday
1 1-3 Lac.Prac. 4-5:50 TAL 350 (Quiz #3) * Fall Housing App Due 4/12	2 Lacrosse at Cent.Conn. (Bus leaves @ 1:30)	3 9-11 Lac.Prac. 12-2 YMCA Internship	4 Free Day!	5 3:30-6 TAL 351 (HW due – Obs.#3)	6 1-3 Lac. Prac. 4-5:50 TAL 350 6:30-9 PE 153 (Lesson Plan Due)	7 7-9 Lac. Prac. 8:30-9:45 PE 170 3:15-5:45 TAL 407 8-9 Study Hall
8 3- Lacrosse @ Sacred Heart PE 170 (HW Session 8)	9 7-9 Lac. Prac. 4-6:30 TAL 399 * schedule Fall Reg. Advisement	10 1-Lacrosse @ Quin. 4-8 YMCA Internship	11 Free Day!	12 8:30-2 PS 261 Observation 3:30-6 TAL 351	13 8:30-10:30 TAL 359.1 4-5:50 TAL 350 6:30-9 PE 153 (project #4 due)	14 7-9 Lac. Prac. 8:30-9:45 PE 170 3:15-5:45 TAL 407 8-9 Study Hall
15 1-3 Lac.Prac. 4-5:50 TAL 350 PE 170 (HW session 9)	16 7-9 Lac Prac. 4-6:30 TAL 399	17 9-11 Lac. Prac. 12-8 YMCA Internship	18 Concert Asbury Park – Skate & Surf Festival	19 8:30-2 PS 261 Obs. 3:30-6 TAL 351 (Group Presentation)	20 8:30-10:30 TAL 359.1 4:00-5:50 TAL 350 6:30-9 PE 153 (Jour.#5 due)	21 7-9 Lac. Prac. 8:30-9:45 PE170 3:15-5:45 TAL 407
22 1-3 Lac.Prac. 4-5:50 TAL 350 PE 170 (HW session 10)	23 3- Lacrosse @ S.F. 4-6:30 TAL 399	24 9-11 Lac. Prac. 12-8 YMCA Soccer Tournament Stony Brook----->	25 Soccer Tournament	26 3:30-6 TAL 351 (Group Presentation) * Immunization recs. due to Health Svcs.	27 8:30-10:30 TAL 359.1 4-5:50 TAL 350 6:30-9 PE 153 (Child Study paper due)	28 8:30-9:45 PE 170 3:15-5:45 TAL 407 (Final Exam)
29 4-5:50 TAL 350 (Quiz #4 & Journal #6 due)	30 4-6:30 TAL 399 2-2:30 Fall Reg. Advisement	31				

Tina is a two-sport student-athlete (soccer, lacrosse) majoring in physical education.

Figure 4.2 Weekly Schedule

March/April	Sun 3/28	Mon 3/29	Tues 3/30	Wed 3/31	Thurs 4/1	Fri 4/2	Sat 4/3
6 AM / 6:30		Wake-up	Wake-up ------------ Morning Jog	Wake-up ------------ Morning Jog			
7 / 7:30		Morning Jog/Stretch	Clean-up and Breakfast	↓	Wake-up ------------ Breakfast		
8 / 8:30	Wake-up ------------ Breakfast	Weight Room	Earth School Observ. in New York City	Drug Testing Training Room	Depart for Duke	------------ Wake up	Wake-up -------------- Bkfst. Hotel
9 / 9:30	CHURCH	Breakfast	& travel	Weight Room -------------- Breakfast	**(take Soc Books)!	Breakfast at Hotel	Depart for Meet
10		Nap		Fall Advisement		Depart for Meet	
11		Prep. Soc.		Prep. Soc.		(Not running but support team at Meet)	**Run Open 800 m Dash
12		SWK 101	Soc 132	SWK 101			
1 / 1:30	Lunch w. Team -- LIU Café	TAL 301	Lunch	TAL 301			
2 / 2:30	Soc 116 Rd	Quick Bite & Study	Training Room & Practice	Meet with Sociology Chair @ Dept			
3	Chapt & Write 5 Response						
4	Questions			Late Jog and Stretch			
5 / 5:30	TV	Clean-up & Dinner	Clean up & Dinner	Clean up ------------ Start Soc 116			
6 / 6:30	Dinner	Soc 116		Outline & Highlight	Check in & Unpack		Dinner
7 / 7:30	Begin TAL 301 paper		Video Games	Laundry & hang out w. Tali	Practice at Track	Dinner @ Applebees	Depart for NY
8 / 8:30	Video Games	Hang out w. Tali	Finish TAL 301 Paper		Dinner	Pack for Meet	
9 / 9:30	TV				------------ Hang out w. T.	TV ------------ **BED EARLY!	**Study for Soc 116 Exam!
10	TV		Hang out w. Tali				
11	BED	BED	BED	Dinner Chinese Take-Out	BED		
12 AM / 12:30				BED			BED

Isaiah is a teaching and learning major and student-athlete in track and field.

Figure 4.3 Daily Schedule on 3 by 5 Index Card

6-7:30	wake up	5:30	dinner & nap
	shower		
	breakfast	7	coffee w. Sara
7:30-8:45	study for quiz	8	library study
9	class—quiz	10	dorm study
11-1:30	training room	1	bed
	shower		
1:30	class (take lunch)		

Sonia is a physical therapy major and student-athlete in softball.

USE YOUR PLANNER ACTIVELY. Make sure your planner, organizer, or to-do list is close at hand and easy to find at all times. No matter how neat and well organized, a planner that's buried under a pile of paper on your desk or hidden under your bed isn't any help. Be sure to refer to it regularly. Too many students have everything neatly written out but forget to look at it. So keep your planner open to the appropriate day, week, or month whenever you're in your room. And when you go out, take it with you so you can use it actively and check it before committing to something new that might conflict with an already scheduled activity. Also, make your entries in pencil or erasable marker so that if or when things change, as they so often do, you can easily make revisions.

VISUALIZE THE COMING DAY. Think about what lies ahead and what you need to accomplish. This will help you take control of the day, rather than feeling like it's controlling you.

> Every night before going to bed I take a moment to jot down a schedule for the following day. I include wake-up time, meals, classes, practices, homework, naps, any errands I have to run, phone calls I have to make, etc. And then I stick to it. This helps me not only to get everything done but is instrumental in staying focused throughout the day. If you want to watch soap operas, that's fine. But put it in the schedule.
>
> — Dan Bradley

> At the beginning of the day I think ahead and go through my day hour by hour and tell myself what I would like to accomplish that day. And then, when that time comes, it's important to stay focused and complete the task.
>
> — Spencer Harris

I KNOW IT'S AROUND HERE SOMEWHERE. Looking for things you need but can't find is a waste of time. So get organized! Get hold of some file folders or large envelopes and dedicate a space to keep them in. Developing a filing system for important school-related as well as personal records and papers will save you time. You might want to have separate folders for course registration, grades and transcripts, bills and receipts, financial aid, housing and other contracts, health insurance, and course materials.

IS IT WORKING? Schedules are not etched in stone. Every so often, ideally early in the semester, take time for reflection. Honestly ask yourself how your schedule feels. Is it working? Have your time estimates been realistic and accurate? Take control! Go ahead and revise the schedule in ways that will make it work better for you.

 ## Making the Most of Your Time

SET PRIORITIES AND STICK TO THEM. It's easy to get off track doing things that are more fun but less important. In fact, some students find that doing tasks they *don't* like first helps them avoid procrastinating. And they don't walk around all day dreading what they have to do later.

> I do not look at it as juggling both athletics and academics because I take care of all academics first and then team obligations. I look at it like this: I want to have something to take with me when I leave besides just great memories.
>
> — Abraham Billy Hardee III
>
> Most importantly, I realize that I am first a student and then an athlete. I always put my academics first and find time for everything else after that.
>
> — Jill Firman

TAKE ADVANTAGE OF YOUR BREAKS. Use the time before and after classes to take care of what you have to do. This is especially useful if you have long breaks between classes. Extended between-class breaks are a very good time to study and review notes or to sit down and eat a full meal, rather than gobbling something down on the run.

MULTITASKING HELPS. Many of the things you do every day require that you be at a certain place but don't require your full attention the whole time you're there. So bring along a textbook or your class notes and use the time productively, by getting assigned reading done or by studying.

> As a student-athlete I had to keep in mind that I had a lot to do in very little time. Therefore, I would use laundry time or time on the campus bus as additional study time. If necessary, I used the time I had in the training room (e.g., ice bath, heat) for studying. Times like these, although small, help a great deal in accomplishing an academic goal.
>
> — Courtney Turner

TIME-OUT!

Interview a student-athlete who always seems to get everything done. How does he or she do it? How can *you* do it?

SWITCHING GEARS CAN BE TOUGH. So when you plan your time, be sure to be realistic about how tired you'll be after practice or how hard it will be to focus on studies before or after a game, meet, or other competition.

> The most difficult part of being a student-athlete is that after a day of classes, a grueling practice, and returning to your room at 7 o'clock, the last thing you want to do is study.
>
> — Becky Hunnewell

MAKE LARGE TASKS FEEL SMALLER. Break down seemingly overwhelming tasks into more manageable, less intimidating pieces that feel (and are) more doable. For example, if you have to read 30 pages in a dry textbook, don't focus on having to get through the whole 30-page assignment. Aim to bite off 15 pages, take a short break, and then return for the rest.

> Don't let yourself get overwhelmed by what lies in front of you. If you have a big project, break it down into smaller steps that are much easier to concentrate on. Or if you have two games and two tests this week, don't worry about all four things at once. Instead, spend time preparing for only one of your tests at a time. When you are at practice or a game, don't think about your work. Concentrate on what is in front of you at the moment. Also, planning out events in advance and spreading them out over a period of time generally takes stress away as well. However, procrastinating usually causes a big headache.
>
> — Jim Olds

MAKE WEEKENDS WORK. Time management isn't only about Monday through Friday. Be sure to plan your weekends the same way you do weekdays. Of course, Saturdays and Sundays may be great for catching up on much needed sleep or your social life, but the more productively you use weekend time, the easier your weekdays will be.

> Weekends are a great time to study. We are not like normal students who can relax after a week of schoolwork. Student-athletes must use this time to do schoolwork.
>
> — Becky Hunnewell

IT'S OKAY TO SAY "NO." Avoid getting too involved and overextended. At times, when there is just too much going on and you feel pulled in too many different directions, it may not be a bad idea to say you're sorry, but you just can't.

PLAN TO DO NOTHING. For better or worse, you're only human, not a superhero or superheroine. You can't function effectively if you're always on the go. So make certain you set aside and plan for "do-nothing" time—not whenever you feel like it but built into your schedule.

> With all the time that you give to your sport and your studies, you have to set aside some time for yourself, and only yourself. Having some silent time alone where you allow yourself to rejuvenate will help you stay on track and help prevent burnout.
>
> — Lauren Fendrick

> Sometimes you just have to make yourself study when others are out with friends. This is not to say that you have to give up a social life. Make sure you set time aside each week to let yourself relax and have fun.
>
> — Royce Ramey

IT'S *NOT* OKAY TO PROCRASTINATE. As we said previously, doing nothing is fine. But don't procrastinate. To have the luxury of that "do-nothing" time, you've got to set up your schedule so you start working on assignments as soon as you get them. Ignoring assignments doesn't make them go away. It just makes it more difficult to do them well and hand them in on time.

TIME-OUT!

List four ways you waste time. In the next week, take steps to eliminate two of them.

YOU *CAN* TAKE IT WITH YOU. Of course, you always want to have as much of your academics completed as you can before traveling to away events. But when you can't get it all done, you'll need to make the best possible use of time spent traveling and staying overnight away from campus. Plan in advance, so you know what assignments are due when you return, and be sure to take the materials you'll need to complete those assignments with you. Also, if you can, take along a laptop computer to work on any papers that might be coming due. (Ask around because some Athletics Departments have loaners available.) Instead of just hanging around waiting for flights, use the time to look through flash cards in preparation for upcoming exams. Reading or studying on a bus or plane isn't easy, but it can be done if you're able to block out distractions. Sometimes listening to music through headphones can help. In addition, hotel rooms can provide quiet environments in which to study and get work done. Ask to room with a teammate who shares your commitment to academics. But be realistic. You probably won't be able to accomplish much just before meet or game time, or when you're tired, or too upset, hyped, or elated about your performance.

> I always read on the bus. Whether it's a 6-hour trip to Maine or Philadelphia or we leave school at 6:30 a.m., my mentality is "I'm up, so I might as well get something done."
>
> — Doug White

TEAM OBLIGATIONS AREN'T A VALID EXCUSE. Of course there are times when you feel overwhelmed by all that playing a sport involves. But not fulfilling your academic responsibilities because of too many team responsibilities is not acceptable.

> There *will* be times when the stress mounts and it seems like there is not enough time for schoolwork, but there usually is. Sometimes I had to accept that there was simply not as much time as I would have liked to complete a project. But at the same time I told myself that this should not be an excuse to stop caring.
>
> — David Ledet

TALK WITH YOUR COACH. When you feel overwhelmed and *before* your academics are in jeopardy, don't be afraid to discuss the situation with your coaches. They know how important it is for you to succeed in the classroom, and they truly want you to do well.

> If things get too hectic, consider asking your coach to help by allowing you to take a day off or reschedule practice (easier if you are in an individual-type sport, e.g., track, tennis).
>
> — Angela Whyte

DON'T BE A GYM RAT WHEN THERE'S SCHOOLWORK TO BE DONE. Be careful about spending an excessive amount of time hanging out in the gym or conditioning room. Keep to your schedule. Minimize distractions.

> Put limits on yourself for the amount of time you'll spend at the gym because it's easy to get caught up extending practice time into continuous social time.
>
> — Mariko Tansey Holbrook

THE SOONER YOU START, THE BETTER. Start writing, researching, or studying for exams as far in advance as possible. If you don't, you're likely to find yourself behind the eight ball trying to get the work done at the last minute, at the end of a long day when you feel exhausted. And then whatever you manage to get done will be less than your best, if it's acceptable at all.

A FINAL WORD. As a student-athlete, balancing what you have to do with what you have time to do will be a critical factor in determining your success both as a student and as an athlete. And it will help you have more fun, too. It requires planning, commitment, focus, and discipline, the same qualities it took to become the athlete you are today. It comes down to this question: Do you want to do it? It's certainly worth the effort. How well you manage time will, in many ways, determine whether your next 4 or 5 years will be enjoyable and rewarding or a burdensome, unsatisfying chore. You deserve to have fun and feel good about yourself. And what's more, your ability to manage time efficiently will stay with you long after you leave college. You'll reap the benefits for the rest of your life.

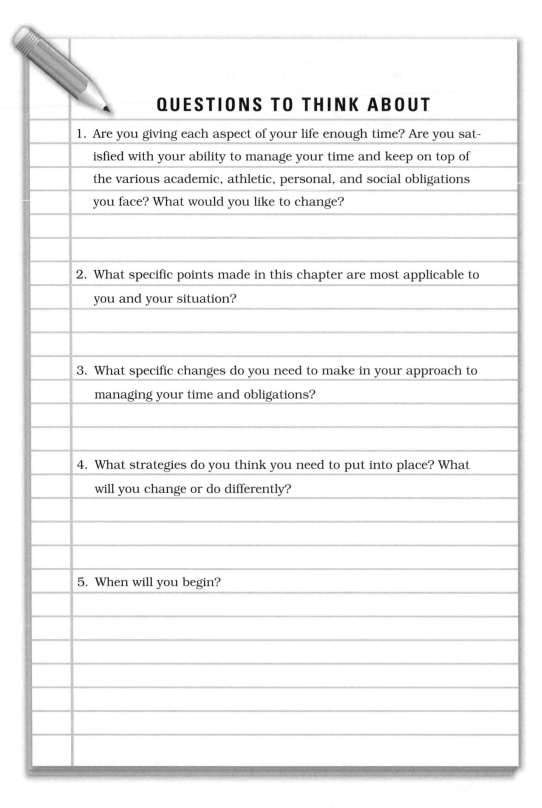

QUESTIONS TO THINK ABOUT

1. Are you giving each aspect of your life enough time? Are you satisfied with your ability to manage your time and keep on top of the various academic, athletic, personal, and social obligations you face? What would you like to change?

2. What specific points made in this chapter are most applicable to you and your situation?

3. What specific changes do you need to make in your approach to managing your time and obligations?

4. What strategies do you think you need to put into place? What will you change or do differently?

5. When will you begin?

Monthly Schedule

NAME OF MONTH:

1	2	3	4	5	6	7
8	9	10	11	12	13	14
15	16	17	18	19	20	21
22	23	24	25	26	27	28
29	30	31				

Note: In the shaded area above, write the appropriate days of the week for the month you are planning, e.g., "Thursday," "Friday," etc.

Monthly Schedule

NAME OF MONTH:

1	2	3	4	5	6	7
8	9	10	11	12	13	14
15	16	17	18	19	20	21
22	23	24	25	26	27	28
29	30	31				

Note: In the shaded area above, write the appropriate days of the week for the month you are planning, e.g., "Thursday," "Friday," etc.

Weekly Schedule

	Sun	Mon	Tues	Wed	Thurs	Fri	Sat
6 AM							
6:30							
7							
7:30							
8							
8:30							
9							
9:30							
10							
10:30							
11							
11:30							
Noon							
12:30							
1							
1:30							
2							
2:30							
3							
3:30							
4							
4:30							
5							
5:30							
6							
6:30							
7							
7:30							
8							
8:30							
9							
9:30							
10							
10:30							
11							
11:30							
12 AM							
12:30							

Weekly Schedule

	Sun	Mon	Tues	Wed	Thurs	Fri	Sat
6 AM							
6:30							
7							
7:30							
8							
8:30							
9							
9:30							
10							
10:30							
11							
11:30							
Noon							
12:30							
1							
1:30							
2							
2:30							
3							
3:30							
4							
4:30							
5							
5:30							
6							
6:30							
7							
7:30							
8							
8:30							
9							
9:30							
10							
10:30							
11							
11:30							
12 AM							
12:30							

CHAPTER 5

Scheduling for Success and for Enjoyment

I chose classes based on my degree of interest rather than their degree of difficulty. It's not work if you enjoy it.

— David Ledet

You just read about the importance of managing your time and learned strategies you might use to do so. In many ways, time management begins with your academic program: the courses you choose, the days and times you choose to take them, and the professors you take them with. That's because in college, students are pretty much in charge of making up their own academic schedule, which can be more difficult than it sounds.

You will probably be given all kinds of advice from well-meaning friends, teammates, roommates, and academic advisors about selecting and scheduling classes. Perhaps even aunts and uncles will have something supposedly helpful to say.

Some will recommend that you get all your core requirements out of the way as quickly as possible and then take electives. Others will say that in your first few semesters you shouldn't register for large lecture classes (as core courses tend to be) but rather take classes with smaller enrollments where you can get to know the professors better. You'll be told that it's best to start your day bright and early by taking an 8 a.m. class. But you may also hear that it's a bad idea to take a class so early. You may be advised to sign up for rigorous courses because you'll get more from them, but also hear that it's a bad idea because there's no need to burden yourself with all that extra work. Some will advise you to register for only 12 credits and not kill yourself; others will insist you're better off signing up for 15 credits and keeping your options open if you don't like a class and want to drop it.

"Avoid heavy reading courses, heavy writing courses, and courses with weekly quizzes." "Professor XYZ is terrible." "No, you've got to take Prof XYZ, he's the best."

Here's the bottom line: The courses you select each semester, as well as the days and times you take them, are important decisions. They can have a huge impact in determining whether you will find your next 4 or 5 years to be manageable, as well as intellectually broadening, and fun. But again, to become an athlete good enough to compete at the college level, you made choices and didn't take the easy way out. You believed that when it comes to athletic performance, "You get out of it what you put into it." It's the same when it comes to being a successful college student. There are tough choices to make, and *you* have to make them. This chapter will help.

Tips from Peers and Profs

Understanding the Process and Taking Control

BE ACTIVE. It is essential that you become active in the academic advisement process and maintain control over what is happening with your schedule. Make sure your advisors in both the Athletics Department and your major department get to know you personally. Share with them what interests you academically as well as your long-term goals. Be sure to tell them how you learn best and what you find exciting and challenging. Don't leave everything in their hands or expect them to take care of everything and hand you a schedule without your input. Do your own academic planning, prepare your own agenda, and have questions ready *before* consulting with advisors. And don't wait for the last minute (or later) to do it!

BEGIN WITH THE COLLEGE CATALOG. Available in hard copy and, at many schools, on CD and online, the catalog or bulletin explains everything you need to know about your college's academic requirements and regulations. (Keep a hard copy from the year you were admitted because it lays out the requirements that you and the school must follow, even if they are revised for future entering classes.) For example, as a freshman or sophomore, you probably won't be allowed to enroll in whatever classes you wish. Like all students, you'll most likely have to complete core curriculum requirements and prerequisite courses before being allowed to take advanced classes.

The catalog will also tell you which courses and how many credits you'll have to take before you'll be eligible to declare a major or minor in specific fields of study. In addition, it contains course descriptions, as well as information related to adding or dropping courses, computation of GPA, grade appeals and reevaluation, and course withdrawal procedures. Especially helpful is the sample semester-by-semester program taken by a typical student in each major. You may also find a listing of the semesters when courses are regularly offered. This gives you an idea of what the next 3 or 4 academic years may look like. Of course, if something isn't clear to you, be sure to ask your academic advisor for help.

TIME-OUT!

Pick up a copy of the catalog or bulletin. Select an area you *might* major in, and list the prerequisite courses that must be completed before you can declare it as your major. When and how often are these courses offered?

CHECK THE CLASS/COURSE SCHEDULE. Published by the registrar and available in print or online a few months before the start of each semester, the class/course schedule lists all courses (as well as the days and times) that will be offered in the upcoming semester. You may notice that sometimes a number of sections of the same course will be listed, meeting on different days of the week and at different times. The names of faculty tentatively assigned to teach each section may also be listed. But this can change, so check with the academic department for the most up-to-date faculty assignments. This information can help you tailor your schedule so it works best with your academic needs and athletic demands. In addition, be aware that not every course is offered every semester. So when planning your schedule, think about scheduling beyond the upcoming semester, and take into consideration how frequently the courses you may need will be offered. The schedule also includes your college's academic calendar of important dates (holidays and school breaks, exam periods, deadlines for adding or withdrawing from courses, etc.). Be sure to mark these in your monthly planner.

BE AWARE OF SPECIAL REQUIREMENTS FOR ATHLETES. Your college, the athletic conference in which you compete, and the NCAA or other governing bodies all have standards that you must meet to practice and compete. So, as an athlete, you also need to have a copy of your school's *Student-Athlete Handbook* or *Guidelines for Maintaining Academic Eligibility for Intercollegiate Practice and Competition.* In it you'll find vital information regarding academic progress, academic standing, full-time enrollment, declaration of major and degree program, minimum degree requirements based on year of enrollment, seasons of eligibility, and minimum GPA requirements.

TIME-OUT!

Carefully review your *Student-Athlete Handbook.* Make a list of your academic obligations. Go over the list with your Academic Advisor for Athletes to be sure you haven't missed anything.

Avoiding Procrastination

STICK TO DEADLINES. Make certain you closely follow all advisement, registration, withdrawal, and financial aid procedures as they are specified in the catalog and handbook. And be sure to do things well in advance of the deadlines listed. Don't wait for the last minute. Although as an athlete you may have different deadlines than the general student body, they are deadlines nonetheless. And it's your responsibility to adhere to them.

BE PROACTIVE. Check your school's academic calendar, and take note of important dates for advisement, preregistration, and registration. Record these dates on your monthly planner. Always meet with your advisors and preregister as early as possible to avoid getting closed out of courses or having course conflicts. If you do get closed out of a class you need or really want to take, try speaking with the professor scheduled to teach it or with the department chairperson. Let him or her know how much you'd appreciate the opportunity to be in the class. Often, there's room for one more student but the registrar's computer doesn't show it.

TALK ABOUT IT. Meet with your advisors, especially your Academic Advisor for Athletes, several times a semester, not just at the last minute on the final day of registration for a quick signature on your program card. This is important because it gives them the opportunity to monitor how you're doing, confirm that you're interpreting your school's academic and athletic regulations properly, and ensure that you're making adequate progress toward your degree.

 TIME-OUT!

> When does registration for next semester begin? Make an appointment to meet with your Academic Advisor for Athletes and any other assigned academic advisor well before then. Be sure to note the dates and times of the appointments on your planner.

Taking Account of Your Personal Style, Needs, and Preferences

WHAT EXCITES YOU? Take meaningful courses that represent more than just another three or four credits and a grade. Actively seek out and register for courses that will engage and excite you and connect with your personal interests. As much as you can, avoid taking only large lecture classes where students may tend to sit passively, take notes, and have little, if any, interaction with professors or classmates. This won't always be possible, especially when you're taking required courses at large universities. But, in general, smaller is better.

> Don't take a class because half your team has taken it and they have the notes and old tests.
>
> — Dan Bradley

GET THE INSIDE SCOOP. Ask advisors, faculty, and other students (athletes and nonathletes), especially those who do well academically and have been on campus for a while, for their suggestions about really good professors whose classes will be both educationally enriching and enjoyable. Inquire about which professors are more flexible. Given student-athletes' competition and travel schedules that might conflict with class attendance, faculty members who are accommodating can make a difference. In addition, many schools have students evaluate courses and faculty each semester according to a variety of criteria. Check these out, but remember, the professor who has a reputation as the easiest grader on campus isn't necessarily the best professor. And the big-name, world-famous professor isn't always the best classroom teacher. Along the same lines, don't simply rely on how a course is described in the catalog. A good professor can make a dull-sounding course exciting, and a poor professor can turn a potentially enjoyable course into a real yawner.

> Talk to upperclassmen and make relationships with athletes from other sports. Chances are they have input that would greatly affect your class selection and schedule setup.
>
> — Jason Roberts

TIME-OUT!

Ask five upper-class teammates and five upper-class nonathletes to name the three best professors on campus and the three best courses. Write down their answers and look for those named often. Ask your advisors when you will be able to register for them.

BE REALISTIC. To get off on the right foot as a freshman, you want to be careful not to overburden yourself academically. But remember, you must take a minimum number of credits to maintain your athletic eligibility. Also begin to chip away at your degree requirements while having as enjoyable an educational experience as possible. Be sure to speak with your Academic

Advisor for Athletes about setting up a manageable academic program, especially in your first and second semesters.

AIM FOR A BALANCED WORKLOAD. Different courses, and even different sections of the same course, can require vastly different types and amounts of work. So once you've identified courses you'd like to take and determined they're available, try to anticipate what the workload will be like and whether it will be manageable. The best way to do that is to speak with students who have taken the courses with the professors scheduled to teach them and to review the syllabi. Check online to see if the syllabi are posted, or visit the academic departments and ask the professors who will be teaching the classes or the department secretaries if you could review the course syllabi that will be used or the ones the professors most recently used. Then try to get a sense of what each of the courses you are considering will require of you and how well they fit together as a whole. For example, how much and what type of reading will you have to do for each course? Rather than five reading-intensive courses, would it be more manageable to take three heavy reading courses and two that are less focused on reading? What kinds of assignments and exams will there be? Will lengthy research papers be required? Intensive memorization? What about additional fieldwork, internship, or laboratory hours? But don't reject a course just because it looks like it will be challenging. Use the answers to these types of questions to put together a balanced schedule that will allow you to manage your time and do your best in all your classes, even the most challenging ones.

LOOK AT THE BIG PICTURE. Create several possible schedules, listing days and times of classes, along with adequate time for meals and studying (see Figure 4.2, and use the sample forms at the end of chapter 4). Consider your athletic obligations: in-season practice and competition schedules, travel periods, and off-season training and practice schedules. What do the days look like? How will they feel? Are you going to have three classes in a row, with no break for lunch? Are the classes spread so far out on campus that it will be difficult, if not impossible, to get to them on time? Will your team's travel or practice schedule conflict with a class? Discuss these hypothetical schedules with your academic advisor, and get feedback on which appears to be the most manageable. Remember, it doesn't matter whether it works or doesn't work for your friends and teammates. It has to work for *you.*

Organizing your class schedule prior to registration is very important. Also, getting into a "groove" of when and how you accomplish daily events will help you be more successful. . . . I've found success by taking the majority, if not all, of my classes, on two days (a third day, if necessary). By using the "block" technique, I found myself more focused on class those 2 days. The days prior to class day are free for studying and reviewing. This type of schedule also leaves room for fulfilling team obligations, extracurricular activities, and helps prevent missed classes.

— Tim Donnelly

When picking classes, be sure to leave room in your schedule for meals. It is also helpful to have a short break between your classes and any practices. This will allow you to unwind and relax before you need to change your focus to athletics.

— Seth Neumuller

TIME-OUT!

Review the class/course schedule for next semester, and create three possible schedules. Ask a senior teammate who does well academically and manages time well to provide feedback on them.

YOU'RE NOT A MACHINE. Keep in mind that Seth Neumuller's advice is equally applicable in the other direction as well: Be sure you have time to unwind and relax *after* practice or a workout and *before* attending a class, hitting the books, or attending to assignments.

TRY TO MINIMIZE CONFLICTS. Unfortunately, it's virtually impossible to end up with a perfect schedule, one that allows you to fulfill all your academic and athletic obligations comfortably and without conflicts. But to the greatest extent possible, try to ensure that your athletic and academic schedules accommodate each other. At times there will be conflicts between the two, which will call for decision making on your part. Consult with your professors, Academic Advisor for Athletes, and your coach in an effort to balance competing academic and athletic demands.

Try to be flexible and innovative with practice time. Don't get so carried away with arranging your classes around practice that you miss out on some incredible class experiences. This is more difficult if you play a team sport, but you could still lift or do individual drills at an alternate time in order to attend a certain class.

— Mariko Tansey Holbrook

Maximizing Your Options

YES, YOU CAN DROP A CLASS. If you attend the first meeting of a class and it feels problematic, you may not have to stick it out. Speak with your Academic Advisor for Athletes immediately about dropping the class, changing sections, or enrolling in a different course.

For a freshman coming in, I suggest they register for 15 hours with the intent of dropping one class if necessary. This gives you some flexibility to discard a class that you feel you may not enjoy. Twelve hours is plenty for freshmen until they get oriented to their new lifestyle.

— Royce Ramey

DIFFERENT STROKES. For some student-athletes, the off-season (if there is one) is a time to register for a heavier course load because there are fewer athletic obligations. Others find that during their competition season they are more efficient and make better use of their time, so they're able to handle extra classes or more difficult ones. Obviously, these result in different approaches to constructing academic schedules. There's no one right way to proceed. Take morning classes? Three 1-hour classes or one 3-hour class? There are no hard and fast rules. As we've said before, what matters is *you*. You have to know yourself and consider realistically what works best for you.

I found I have had my best quarters academically when I have been the busiest. Having a lot of obligations forces me to prioritize and not waste any time.

— Katie Younglove

Take the classes that are most demanding in the off-season when you have more time to commit to schoolwork.

— Angela Whyte

Don't overestimate the amount of time you have in your off-season. I tend to procrastinate more in the off-season because I think I have so much time. However, because I procrastinate, I become more stressed and my grades suffer.

— Patricia Metzger

WHAT ABOUT SUMMER CLASSES? Most colleges and universities offer classes during the summer. Taking them can be a useful way to catch up quickly with credits, but it isn't necessarily a good idea. Taking summer classes can be quite intense. The classes typically meet 4 or 5 days a week for a shortened semester and cover all the material usually covered in a normal 15-week semester. In addition, it's summer, so while you're in class, your friends may be working to pay bills or out at the beach relaxing. And you may want to be doing the same yourself. So think carefully, consider your options, and consult with your Academic Advisor for Athletes before enrolling.

> Since I always had to practice and work, even though I always took a full load, I still had to rely on summer classes. . . . I took what I could during the year but took the more difficult classes during the summer.
>
> — Courtney Turner

COLLEGE IS ABOUT MORE THAN ACADEMICS AND ATHLETICS. Although you have very little free time, consider building into your schedule at least one activity that will be relaxing and fun (e.g., becoming part of a dance or music group, joining the chess club, working at the campus radio or TV station, or volunteering for community service). Many students find these activities not just relaxing and fun, but rewarding as well. You might also consider registering for an elective course, like pottery or photography, that will allow you to enrich and enjoy yourself and earn credits all at the same time.

TIME-OUT!

List three non-sports-related activities you enjoy. How can you build time for them into your schedule? Why should you try?

A CAUTIONARY NOTE. It's unfortunate, but some student-athletes, especially freshmen, have reported that they were placed in unchallenging (to put it mildly) courses. Even worse, some later found out that one or more of these courses couldn't be used toward their degree. Others were encouraged to take an easy course load with supposedly soft-hearted professors or were handed their complete schedule without having any input. Although these are not common occurrences, you need to be cautious. You must understand the academic scheduling process and take control of it, rather than allowing others to control it for you. There really is a lot at stake—your future!

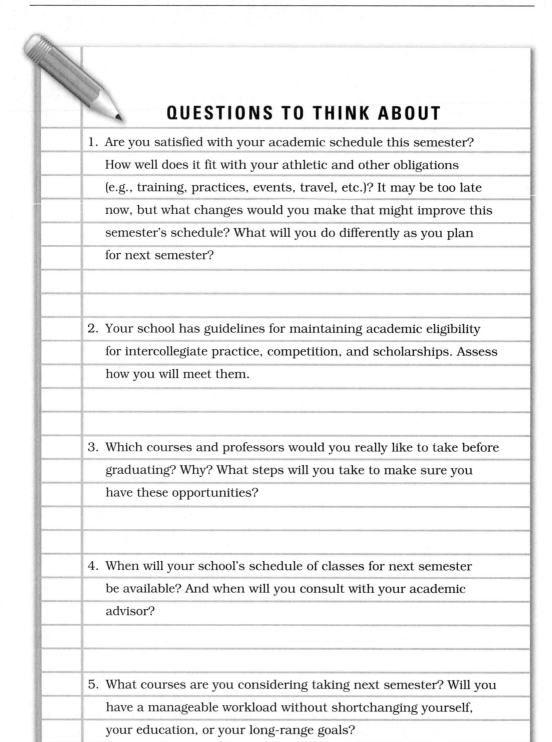

QUESTIONS TO THINK ABOUT

1. Are you satisfied with your academic schedule this semester? How well does it fit with your athletic and other obligations (e.g., training, practices, events, travel, etc.)? It may be too late now, but what changes would you make that might improve this semester's schedule? What will you do differently as you plan for next semester?

2. Your school has guidelines for maintaining academic eligibility for intercollegiate practice, competition, and scholarships. Assess how you will meet them.

3. Which courses and professors would you really like to take before graduating? Why? What steps will you take to make sure you have these opportunities?

4. When will your school's schedule of classes for next semester be available? And when will you consult with your academic advisor?

5. What courses are you considering taking next semester? Will you have a manageable workload without shortchanging yourself, your education, or your long-range goals?

CHAPTER 6

Choosing a Major

What Do You Want to Do with Your Life and How Do You Get There?

> Student-athletes have a different career planning process because they have a talent that may be exploited for large sums of money. The problem is that many athletes put all their hopes into this and do not have a contingency plan. My freshman year I fell into this trap and thought I would just play tennis. But then it hit me: I really needed to use the educational opportunity that I had at my fingertips.
>
> — Royce Ramey

Each year, close to 400,000 student-athletes represent their school in NCAA sports, and many thousands more participate under the auspices of other governing organizations. Like many of these outstanding athletes, you may be hoping, or even expecting, that after your college career is over, you'll sign a lucrative multiyear pro contract and then coach or become a TV sports commentator. Unfortunately, the odds of this happening are quite slim. As we've mentioned before, only slightly more than 1% of college athletes go on to compete professionally. And of those who do, most have professional careers that last less than 5 years. So it's really important that you prepare for what you're going to do vocationally when your competitive career is over.

As Royce Ramey came to realize, attending college offers the educational opportunities you need to prepare for a personally fulfilling future. But unfortunately, too many student-athletes wait until their last year of eligibility (or even after their eligibility has expired), and then they find themselves anxiously thinking, "I have no idea what I'm going to do after graduation." Instead of falling into this trap, we'd like to help you improve the chances that on graduation day you'll be able to say, "I really got out of college what I came for—an education and a promising future."

Although this book is primarily oriented to help you succeed academically, selecting a major and career decision making go hand in hand with academic success. Each has a profound influence on the others. Students do better in courses that relate to their major (assuming they've chosen a major that reflects who they are and what their goals are). It makes sense: When you feel your courses can lead to something beneficial and when they capitalize on your strengths and interests, you're more likely to find them enjoyable. And you're then more likely to be motivated, focused, get more out of them, and earn higher grades. Another benefit is that when you do well and demonstrate interest in a particular faculty member's field, there's a much better chance that he or she will take an interest in your career decision making and assist you with finding an internship or job or getting admitted to graduate or professional school.

It's our hope that before you know it you'll be all decked out in cap and gown, attending your college graduation ceremony. We encourage you to begin immediately to prepare for when that day arrives. Start now to identify your interests and aspirations, and set postcollege goals that reflect them. Then apply the motivation, focus, and commitment that have served you well in your athletic endeavors to achieve those goals.

Tips from Peers and Profs

Consider the Possibilities

SHOOT FOR THE STARS, BUT BE REALISTIC. Having a dream is wonderful. As an athlete, you may dream of earning your livelihood doing something related to your sport. It makes sense! Competing professionally, appearing in commercials, then years later moving on to coaching, being a TV commentator or doing play by play, owning a camp or clinic—what a great life! But unfortunately, dreams don't always come true. Even if you make it to the pros, professional careers are often cut short because of injury, declining ability, others having superior skills, or just plain old bad luck, so only a tiny percentage of college athletes end up living out their dream as pros. That's why you absolutely need to plan for other, ideally equally rewarding possibilities. Your college education is the foundation on which to base that planning.

> Be mature enough to realize that when college is over, being a professional athlete isn't a viable option for the majority of us. So take a moment and confirm that pursuing an education is the real explanation for why you are in college in the first place.
>
> — Seth Neumuller

NO IDEA WHAT YOU WANT TO DO? JOIN THE CROWD! If you have no idea what career to pursue or what to major in, you're certainly not alone. Most entering freshmen don't know what they want to major in. In fact, there are so many undecided students on college campuses that many schools have begun to offer exploratory programs to help with choosing a major and career decision making. The point is, it's all right to be undecided. After all, you don't want to lock in to a major or career path before you've taken the time to explore just who you are, what interests you, and what career possibilities make the most sense. But don't procrastinate. Begin the exploration today!

> Going into college I had only an inkling as to what I might be interested in. When asked by a reporter what I might like to focus my collegiate studies on, I simply replied, "Business, law, or business law."
>
> — Doug White

START THINKING ABOUT CAREER POSSIBILITIES RIGHT AWAY. It's easy to put off thinking about career options until "later." Some student-athletes don't see the importance of beginning to think about careers early on; others see it as a waste of time. Please don't be one of them. Your years on campus will pass incredibly quickly, and before you know it, you'll be graduating. When you do, you'll be far better off if you have a direction and some concrete options and possibilities in hand.

> Academics and career options first, running second. It really has to be this way, no matter how badly student-athletes want to think of themselves as immune from having to consider their future as nonathletes in the real world after college. It's hard to come to grips with the reality that no matter how much they excel in their sport, their carefree days are numbered, and a career other than beating people in races or matches must be chosen.
>
> — Seth Neumuller

> Upon entering college, I dedicated my first year to building a foundation for future success. I wasn't particularly interested in a specific career per se, but I did have an idea where I wanted to be (corporate America). I've seen too many incoming freshmen spend their first year partying and wanting to be part of the in-crowd. Then for the next 3 or 4 years they're playing catch-up. Student-athletes need to understand that what they do from day one drastically affects their future.
>
> — Maurice Yearwood

Explore Who You Are

YOU MIGHT BE SURPRISED. There's a good chance that like many student-athletes, you tend to see yourself primarily in terms of your sport: "I'm a diver," "a golfer," "a tennis player," "an offensive tackle," "a point guard," for example. Of course, you're right, but only to a point. Because you're also much more. In thinking about what career possibilities might make the most sense for you, it's essential to consider who you are as a total person—beyond athletics—and figure out what occupations and types of workplaces will best fit with your values, interests, abilities, and personality.

WHAT DO YOU CARE ABOUT? Your *values* are reflected in those beliefs that are most important to you. In thinking about a career, you must consider them. What are your feelings about being near family and friends, financial security, independence, and leisure time? How important is money to you, and how much of it will you need to live the lifestyle you desire? Do you value travel or staying close to home? Spending time outdoors? How much free time and flexibility in your schedule would you like? Are you interested in working to benefit others and giving back to your community? But remember, values change. So you also must think about what you might value in the future, after you've completed school, and keep those values in mind as you consider what major to choose and career path to follow.

TIME-OUT!

Begin thinking about what's important to you. Respond directly to the questions raised in the text.

WHAT TURNS YOU ON? Ideally, your major and your career choice will be related to your *interests.* So take the time to consider what your likes and dislikes, wants and needs are. What do you enjoy? What do you find personally satisfying? What are you good at? Are you interested in math, technology, science, media, history, helping others, public speaking, dance, making music, or writing? Do you find satisfaction working with children or adults or those who are disadvantaged or have special needs? What do you do for fun? Are you okay with the idea of sitting behind a desk for 8 or more hours a day? Before you can identify a career path that matches your interests, you have to spend the time figuring out what your interests are.

TIME-OUT!

Going along with the questions just asked, what turns *you* on? Make a list.

RECOGNIZE YOUR SPECIAL ABILITIES. In chapter 1, we discussed the range of positive traits and *abilities* you have developed to become a stand-out athlete. For example, focus, leadership skills, perseverance, and the ability to work as part of a team are all qualities that have positive carryover value not only in your studies but in the work world as well. In addition, you also possess a variety of other valuable attributes and abilities that will serve you well in specific majors and careers. At the same time, however, you and everyone else also have weaknesses that might limit your ability to succeed in other majors or career areas. You need to be honest with yourself as you consider how your abilities and weaknesses might affect your performance in your courses and in the workplace.

KNOW THYSELF. What are you like? How do you interact with your environment and those around you? Are you a warm, sensitive person who develops close interpersonal relationships, or do you tend to be aloof? Are you more emotionally stable or explosive? Impulsive or do you fully think things through? Willing to take risks or more safe and conservative? Do you work effectively under stress or have difficulty? Take charge or follow? Your *personality* affects everything you do, including your studies and work. Consider these personality characteristics—along with others— as you think about the major, career, and workplace that will make the most sense for you.

Think About Majors That Mesh with Who You Are and Who You Want to Become

YOU MUST HAVE A MAJOR. Although it can take considerable time to decide on a career direction (and we encourage you to take your time), the NCAA requires that by the beginning of your third year of enrollment as a student-athlete attending a 4-year college, you designate a program of study leading to a specific baccalaureate degree. If your school is not NCAA governed, be sure to inquire about similar requirements that affect you.

WHAT'S A MAJOR? A major is a concentration of courses in a particular discipline (field), or it may be interdisciplinary and combine courses from two or more different disciplines. Some majors lead to specific entry-level jobs on a career path (e.g., accounting, education, social work); others prepare you for a variety of career possibilities (e.g., English, philosophy, sociology). Your school has a wide range of majors to consider, and all of them are listed in the college catalog or bulletin. There you'll also find lists of required courses and prerequisites for each major, number of elective courses permitted, deadline dates, steps to follow in declaring a major, and whether or not students are permitted to declare a double major and/or a minor. Some schools even allow students to create their own majors.

TIME-OUT!

Review your college catalog. Make a list of three majors you think might be consistent with your values, interests, abilities, and personality. What are the requirements to be admitted into each?

A SHORT CONVERSATION WITH YOUR COACH ISN'T ENOUGH. Choosing a major is a decision that could have long-lasting implications. So don't rush it. Selecting a major requires time, information, and serious thought. Use your first year or two on campus researching the possibilities, thinking about and testing out possible majors. Visit the academic departments of the majors on your list. Talk to students who are majoring in the areas you are considering, alumni, and family and friends working in related fields who have contacts with whom you can network. And get hold of available literature, Web sites, and other information.

THE MORE QUESTIONS YOU ASK, THE MORE YOU LEARN. Make a list of questions, and then go out and talk with people. Learn as much as you can, and be ready to add new questions to your list. What is the major about, and what fields and positions is it connected to? What employment opportunities might it open up, and what might the work environments be like? What types of interests and skills are required? What courses will you have to take? How rigorous is the workload? How many years of school are required? Is graduate training expected immediately after you've earned your undergraduate degree? Can you do it part time?

> Sit down with a professor in the department of a major you are interested in and ask lots of questions, including the obvious such as career options and classes. If you can get over the intimidation factor, talking with professors can prove to be a great resource.
>
> — Seth Neumuller

THERE'S ALL SORTS OF HELP AVAILABLE. Right on campus you'll find a wide range of career planning services with names like The Undecided Student Advisement Center or The Career Development Center. At these centers, advisors are available to help assess your skills, aptitudes, and interests, and research fields of study and long-term employment trends. They may also be able to help you test out possible fields of study and employment by arranging for you to participate in informational interviews, off-campus volunteer positions, and summer internships. Counselors at these centers will also be able to suggest library resources and reference materials (e.g., the *Dictionary of Occupational Titles* and the *Occupational Outlook Handbook*) and give you suggestions about a course or two that you might enroll in or audit to test out a possible major. In addition, most career services centers periodically sponsor informational meetings with alumni, workshops, on-campus career fairs, panel discussions, and other special events designed to help with career planning and selecting a major. Check bulletin boards and visit the centers often to find out when these special events will take place (see chapter 3).

> It's crucial to plan ahead for real-world job experience (e.g., internships for summers or the off-season). Try starting with the summer after freshman year, so you'll be exposed to a variety of different possibilities and can at least pick a general direction. Ask yourself, "Do I want to work at a newspaper, a hospital, a hotel, an arena, an accounting firm?"
>
> — Doug White

Set High Academic Goals

THINK FOR YOURSELF. Your parents, coaches, teammates, friends, and acquaintances will have lots of advice for you. They'll say, "Whatever you do, don't major in . . . ," "You'll make a lot of money in . . . ," "You've got to go into the [fill in blank] world," and "Let's stick together; major in what I'm majoring in." All of these suggestions are well intentioned, but you owe it to yourself to make your own thoughtful decisions. Selecting a major and deciding on a career can affect the rest of your life. These decisions are too important to simply leave to others.

> Don't rely on other people's opinions. Trust your own instincts and values. And remember, you may not know when something is right for you, but you *will* know when something is wrong.
>
> — Lauren Fendrick

> Don't rush into something just because your parents want you to do it or because you will make a lot of money. If you pursue something that challenges you and that you enjoy, you will be able to enjoy life to the fullest.
>
> — Royce Ramey

DON'T SELL YOURSELF SHORT. It's unfortunate, but rather than encouraging student-athletes to pursue a challenging major leading to a meaningful degree, some coaches and others may try to make it as simple as possible for athletes to pass their courses, maintain their eligibility, and easily get to training and practice. That may sound great, but ask yourself how valuable an education you'll get that way. So be wary when you're encouraged to sit back and let others take care of everything for you. Be careful, too, about being pressured toward majors that have many independent study classes, courses with questionable academic or long-term value, summer courses taken at other campuses under so-called arranged conditions, and online distance learning courses. You may receive high grades with minimal effort in these classes, but other than keeping you eligible, what will you get out of them? Remember, *your* future is your responsibility: Take control of preparing for it.

YOU'RE NOT LOCKED IN. Once you select a major, you don't have to stick with it your entire college career. It's absolutely fine to change majors. In fact, a majority of college students change majors at least once, and some switch three or four times. Of course, you don't want to do it every other week because each time you switch, you have to fulfill a different set of course requirements and risk having to take additional prerequisites. Because this might result in your having to stay in school longer than 4 years, be aware of progress toward degree (PTD) requirements you must meet as a student-athlete. But you don't have to stick with a major if you aren't happy with it. And remember, your major is only a starting point on a career path that will encompass your lifetime. It's common for graduates to change their career plans after they leave college. And the average person changes careers many times before retiring.

> I was fairly set on English before I started school, but my interest in political science actually was a result of my experience in New York. The attacks of 9/11 factored into my decision to major in poli sci, as did the international atmosphere of the city, my school, and my team.
>
> — David Ledet

QUESTIONS TO THINK ABOUT

1. What do you think you'd like to do after you graduate that doesn't involve turning pro or coaching? What will it take for you to be able to do it?

2. What personal attributes, interests, and values do you possess that will affect your ability to succeed and find fulfillment in the career you'd like to pursue?

3. What college major will best prepare you to enter that career field?

4. If you have no idea what you'd like to do, what steps can you take to explore career possibilities? Where on campus can you turn to get assistance?

5. If you decide your major isn't right for you, what could you do to change it?

CHAPTER 7

Playing to Win in the Classroom

Showing that you are willing to be a student first and an athlete second always makes a great impression.

— Jill Turner

From the moment you step into a classroom on campus, one thing is clear: You're not in high school anymore. In high school, there probably weren't huge lecture halls or classes with 50, 100, or more students. It's possible that you knew almost everyone, and they knew you. Even teachers you never had might have known you or at least known about you. And in each class you probably had friends and teammates to sit with. But when you enter your first college classroom, you may not see a single familiar face. And you might ask yourself a range of questions like these: What kind of class will this be? Will there be a lot of work, or will just putting in "seat time" be enough to pass? Will I be able to keep up? Am I smart enough to be here at all? What's the professor going to be like? What have I gotten myself into?

These kinds of concerns are typical and quite normal. But there are also deeper issues you need to think about as you make the transition from high school to college because, in many ways, being a college student is a whole new ball game. There's far less nurturing and personalized hand holding than you might have become used to in high school. In college classes, students have to take more responsibility for their academic performance. Professors tend to grade students based on the quality of the work they submit rather than on the amount of time and effort that's put into it. However, just as there are things you do as an athlete to please your coaches and demonstrate that you have a winning attitude, there are things you can do as a student to put your best foot forward and "play to win" on the academic playing field—the college classroom.

Playing to win in the classroom goes hand in hand with the positive academic mind-set you read about in chapter 2. We're talking about getting to class on time and being prepared, behaving appropriately in class, listening carefully to what professors and fellow students say, taking meaningful and useful notes, participating actively, and building and maintaining positive relationships with your professors and classmates. Basically, we're talking about good academic behaviors and habits. The point is, just as there are critical behaviors that are necessary to achieve success in your sport, there are verbal and nonverbal behaviors that will have a major impact on the grades you earn in your classes and how beneficial your college experience will prove to be after you graduate.

Tips from Peers and Profs

Winning Classroom Behaviors

ATTEND ALL YOUR CLASSES. At times it may be tempting to try to catch up on sleep and take care of other business (like laundry and getting your hair cut) rather than attend class. But it's dangerous, because the only way to be sure you process all that goes on in class is to be there. If you're not in class you may have difficulty understanding course material or miss hints the professor gives about what will be on an upcoming exam. Moreover, unless you have absolutely no choice, you should *never* miss the class session right before an exam. Being absent, or missing part of a class because you showed up late, may make it harder (and more time consuming) to prepare for exams. And because some professors have a strict attendance policy, and some coaches won't allow athletes to compete in the team's next competition if they inexcusably miss class, you may put your course grade or athletic participation in jeopardy. So follow this simple rule: Attend each and every class unless you have a very good reason to be absent (severe illness, off-campus competition, family emergency). By the way, cutting a class because you need the time to do work for another course is *not* a good reason. When you steal from Peter to pay Paul, as the saying goes, your work in both courses is likely to suffer. And most important, remember that being a student-athlete does *not* automatically entitle you to skip or cut classes because you have a scheduling conflict between your academic and athletic obligations.

> I rarely missed a class. Missing classes or lectures could mean missing the helpful hints professors often gave about exams or what not to worry about when reading the book. Or better yet, that the next class would be canceled!
>
> — Erin McIntyre

GET TO CLASS ON TIME OR, BETTER YET, EARLY. Chances are you don't let anything keep you from getting to your athletic events on time. In fact, to be mentally and physically prepared, you probably make sure you get to practices and competitions early. It's a really good idea to do the same with your classes. When possible, make it a habit to arrive at class at least 5 to 10 minutes before it begins. That will give you a chance to quickly review your notes and mentally prepare, just as you do before competition. You'll be ready to deal with course material the moment class begins. That's important because professors often announce assignments and upcoming examination dates at the very beginning of class. Of course don't arrive on time and then leave the room for 20 minutes immediately after the professor has taken attendance.

IF YOU HAVE TO BE LATE, DON'T BE RUDE. Entering the classroom late can be distracting to other students and annoying to professors. It may disrupt their train of thought, or they may feel they have to repeat what they've already said to get you caught up. Walking across the front of the classroom, tossing your equipment loudly against the wall, rearranging the seats, or climbing over people to get a seat next to a teammate are not wise things to do. It's best to quietly take the first available seat. Then, after class, speak to the professor and apologize for your lateness.

AVOID THE BACK OF THE ROOM. We just mentioned some good reasons to get to class a few minutes early. Another is that if you're early, you'll have your choice of seats. And where you sit can affect your performance. Sitting in the back of the room with your teammates makes it harder to pay attention. You may be tempted to talk about yesterday's game, read the newspaper, copy notes from another class, text-message friends, or eat breakfast while the professor is speaking. So try to select a seat toward the front of the classroom or lecture hall. You'll hear better, see better, have fewer distractions to deal with, and be less likely to zone or nod out. And you'll make a better impression on the professor. You may think the professor won't notice, doesn't care, or doesn't know who you are, but you're probably wrong. You'd be surprised what professors are aware of when it comes time to calculate your course grade.

> I learned to sit toward the front of the class in order to listen more carefully. Also, it helps to make eye contact with the teacher. And try not to sit next to friends who will distract you from being able to listen or who will talk to you during class time.
>
> — Julie Ruff

TIME-OUT!

For the next 2 weeks, sit in the first or second row in all your classes. How does it affect your ability to pay attention and take class notes?

BEING PHYSICALLY PRESENT ISN'T ENOUGH. To actually learn the course material and succeed academically, both your body and mind have to show up for class. It's not about just putting in seat time. You've got to get to class with enough energy to stay awake, alert, and attentive. Class time is not daydream, nap, or text-messaging time. Falling asleep in class (or zoning out) means you're not only missing the topic being covered, but it also sends a message that you aren't interested in the course and lack respect for your professor and fellow students. You also risk a reduction in your grade. So if you feel drowsy during class, quietly leave the room, find a rest room, throw some cold water on your face, do 10 jumping jacks, and quickly return to your seat without disturbing the class. Never strut back into the room 15 or 20 minutes later, munching on a bag of chips!

> Don't sleep in class! Athletes are notorious for this, and the professors know it and tend to stereotype us as lazy and only interested in our sport and not school. Prove them wrong!
>
> — Becky Hunnewell

BE PREPARED FOR EACH CLASS. What do you think would happen if you arrived at practice or competition without your uniform and equipment? Or if your coach and teammates expected you to study the playbook, but you never even opened it? You must be prepared, and if you aren't, you might not be allowed to compete or might even be thrown off the team. In the same way, you must be prepared for each class, with the required work completed. The material covered in class is generally based on the readings and other assignments. If you haven't carefully done the work in advance, you'll have a tougher time understanding the lecture and preparing for exams. So no matter how busy you are, schedule adequate time to prepare for all your classes.

Being prepared also means having the necessary supplies with you in class. Whether it's textbooks and workbooks, pens, pencils, paper for taking notes or making graphs, a specialized calculator, or other technology, it's your responsibility to have whatever you will need.

MAKE A GOOD IMPRESSION. Like it or not, appearance counts. Show your professors you are serious by arriving at class appropriately groomed and dressed, not rolling out of bed and into class carrying a bacon-and-egg sandwich or all sweaty or covered with mud from a hard practice or game. In addition, think about what your posture and facial expressions communicate. Do you look alert, alive, and attentive, or bored, uninterested, and anxious to leave? Just as you want to show your coach that you're into your sport, demonstrate to your professors that you're into their courses and into learning. Also, if your campus culture dictates that hats should not be worn in class, then ditch the hat. And here's a good rule of thumb: no earphones! Put them away before you walk into the room. Of course, always remember to turn off your cell phone, text messager, or iPod before class begins.

> ## TIME-OUT!
>
> After one of your classes this week, write an honest description of the impression you think you made on your professor and fellow students. For example, did you appear prepared or unprepared? Interested or disinterested? What improvements could you make?

IF YOU MUST LEAVE EARLY, DON'T MAKE A SCENE. It shouldn't happen very often, but there may be times when, because of your team's travel schedule or some other unavoidable obligation, you will have to leave a class session before it is over. Because you will know about these situations in advance, you can notify the professor by calling, e-mailing, or leaving a note, or by getting to class extra early and telling the professor why and at what time you will have to leave. If the professor requires a note from the Athletics Department, be sure to provide one. Then take a seat close to the door. When you have to go, don't disrupt the class. Gather your belongings and leave the room as quietly as possible. And before the next class meeting, be sure to speak with classmates to find out what you missed.

Mastering Course Syllabi

ROAD MAP TO AN A. What is the class going to be about? What does the professor expect? How much work will there be? How many exams? When will they be given? Short answer or essay? Any papers? Deadlines? How will the course grade be determined? Do attendance and class participation count? Where is the professor's office? Office hours? E-mail address? Phone number? At the start of each new course, virtually every student wants to know the answers to these, as well as other critical questions. The answers are usually addressed during the first class session when the professor distributes the all-important class syllabus or course outline.

The syllabus is like a road map or set of directions. It tells you where the course will go and what you need to learn to earn the grade you hope for. The professor may or may not review the syllabus or answer questions about it the first time the class meets. But whether he or she does or doesn't, be sure to review it carefully, and ask about anything the syllabus might not specify. After that first class, the professor may never refer to the syllabus again. But the expectation is that you will refer to it regularly, use it to keep up with class assignments, and follow it religiously as it guides you through the next 14 or 15 weeks of the semester.

REMEMBER THAT PLANNER? After the first meeting of each of your classes, review the syllabi you were given and highlight all the important due dates listed.

Then take out your planner and carefully record all quiz and exam dates, assignment due dates, field trips, and other critical dates and times. That way, you'll be able to see how your academic work demands are distributed day to day and week to week, as well as over the semester. The idea is to begin early in the term to take control of your workload—before it takes control of you.

USE IT—DON'T LOSE IT. A syllabus stuck in the bottom of a drawer or in a stack of papers at the back of your notebook and forgotten about is of no help to you. Keep syllabi in a safe and accessible spot where they are easy to get at (e.g., stapled onto the inside front cover of each course notebook). Use them as a resource, and review them each week to make sure you are up to date with readings and other assignments. In the end, your knowledge of what's in each syllabus will have a major impact on your ability to meet professors' expectations, follow their directions, and receive the highest possible grades.

Listening, Note Taking, and Participating

FOCUS, FOCUS, FOCUS! Just as you have to be focused to perform at your best during practice and competition, you must be focused to achieve maximum performance in the classroom. You need to be in the right frame of mind and have the energy to listen carefully to everything that is said in class. Listening involves a lot more than merely hearing what the professor or your classmates say. It requires that you become *actively* involved with what goes on, that you think about what the professor and other students are saying, that you process it in your mind, integrating it with information that has come before and will come later. Listening well is not an easy skill to master. And it can be especially difficult when the professor is a poor lecturer or the material being presented is boring or difficult to understand.

Unfortunately, not all professors are great teachers, and you won't find all your courses entertaining or stimulating. But you still have to learn the material covered. In these cases, being able to focus is critical. As an athlete, you've proven you're capable of focusing under trying conditions. So use this skill in the classroom.

> In the classroom I consider it game time and I challenge myself to pay attention and take the best possible notes I can.
>
> — A. David Alston

GOOD NOTES BEGIN WITH GOOD LISTENING. The goal of note taking is to capture the essential points being made (especially if they represent new learning for you), and to highlight them so you can review and study them later. Actively listening in class will help you take more meaningful notes. And the reverse is true as well. Wanting to take good notes will help you listen more actively and effectively. Being able to listen and take notes at the same time is the key.

Putting the two together will result in true learning that will stay with you long after a test or a course is over.

> Try to focus your attention on the lecture. If you write notes on what is being said, the time will pass more quickly. In a smaller classroom, try and make eye contact with your professor to show you are interested. If the professor looks back at you, you will likely listen with greater interest and do better on assignments and exams. By doing something as simple as paying attention in class, you are giving yourself a heads-up.
>
> — Audra Lissell

TIME-OUT!

Evaluate yourself as a listener. Select one class where you have a hard time maintaining your focus or taking good notes. Honestly identify what factors are creating the problem. List a few things *you* can do to improve the situation.

DEVELOP YOUR OWN NOTE-TAKING STYLE. Class notes are personal. Every student has to learn what works best for him or her. So we can't teach you how to take notes; no book can really do that. But we can assure you that the better prepared you are for a class (having done the assigned reading in advance and reviewed material from the previous classes), the more likely you are to take good notes. Actual note taking, though, as we said, is a question of personal style. The key is using as few words as possible to quickly record the professor's main points in your own words. You have to experiment and figure out the method that best fits your learning style. But whatever method you eventually adopt, you will need to develop your own abbreviated shorthand and format that saves time and allows you to keep up with the lecture. Remember, you can't (nor would you want to) write down every word that is said, nor do you want to spell out every long word.

> Taking notes is very individualized. It is important to know your own style and what works for you. I find it very difficult to study from another student's notes. After all, his/her notes are not organized the way my mind thinks. My advice: Figure out what works for you, and go with it.
>
> — Patricia Metzger

PICK UP ON CUES. It's not always easy to know what's important enough to write down in your notes. But if you pay attention, you'll often find that your professors will signal—sometimes verbally, sometimes nonverbally—that what they are about to say is particularly important. Look for professors to repeat key points, spell out technical terms, or put key words on the board; focus on an overhead; or speak louder and more slowly to emphasize a critical point. Also pay special attention when they begin a sentence with phrases like, "The most important . . . ," "I want to stress . . . ," "There are three reasons . . . ," or "I expect you to read . . . and think about . . ." Sometimes they'll come right out and say, "Don't be surprised to find a question on your next exam that asks about . . ." And be alert for statements that begin with words like "Therefore," "Thus," and "In summary." You might then underline or highlight those notes that seem most important. Some professors also post notes or lecture outlines online. Review them, and use them to prepare for the upcoming lecture, or exam, or to clarify and fill in gaps in your own notes, *but not as a substitute for taking your own notes.*

CONNECT WHAT'S SAID IN CLASS TO WHAT YOU READ. The two often go hand in hand. Typically, lectures and class discussions reinforce, clarify, or fill in gaps in the assigned readings. Staying on top of those readings will enable you to make better sense of what's said in class, take better notes, and make the information presented easier to remember and recall at exam time. Also, some professors tend to follow the textbook as they lecture or even lecture straight from the text, so you may want to bring the book to class and mark the critical points. Of course, if the professor requires or suggests that you have the text with you, be sure to bring it.

> I remember my first day of anatomy class when the professor made the point that "The psoas originates on the lumbar vertebrae and inserts on the lesser trochanter." All I could think of was *Whoa!* Am I supposed to be able to understand that? But I realized that the professor's lecture is often a summary of important points in the readings. And when I went to the text, the diagrams and pictures were right there.
>
> — Patricia Metzger

PRACTICE AND DETERMINATION PAY OFF. Note taking is a critical but often difficult skill to master. Just like becoming proficient at your sport, it takes practice and determination to do it well. So if you are having difficulty, don't give up. Seek help from your academic advisor, or attend a note-taking workshop on campus. You might also consider asking your professors' permission to tape-record class sessions as a backup to your notes. After class you can listen to the tapes and make sure your notes are complete. But remember, tapes are not a substitute for class notes, so do both.

BE AN ACTIVE LEARNER. Think seriously about what's being said. Don't just sit back in class and expect to be spoon-fed. In some courses, the professor delivers a lecture and leaves without taking any questions or offering clarification. In these classes, students' questions and comments are often dealt with in smaller sections run by teaching assistants (TAs), through e-mail, or during office hours. Some professors take a few questions before departing; others open each class session by asking students if they have any questions. Then there are professors, especially in smaller classes, who encourage active student participation and factor the quality of your class participation into your final grade. But no matter how your professor structures the class, whenever you have the opportunity, participate actively and thoughtfully. Push yourself to agree or disagree, and to ask and answer questions. Make sure, however, you do so appropriately. And be careful. Don't talk just for the sake of talking or being noticed. Try not to dominate class discussions or question-and-answer periods. Also, professors don't appreciate students repeating a question that was previously asked and answered.

> I sit in the front of *every* class that I am in, and I am not afraid to ask questions.
>
> — Abraham Billy Hardee III
>
> Participate! Teachers love it when students ask and answer questions during a lecture. Sit closer to the front and go to *every* lecture!
>
> — Erin McIntyre

WHEN IT'S NOT COMING FROM THE PROF. Just because someone other than the professor is speaking doesn't mean it's not important. When other students ask questions or make comments, it's your responsibility to listen. It's crucial that you pay attention to everything said in class, no matter who says it. Don't interrupt others' comments. And don't space out when it's not the professor speaking because if you do, you risk missing not only what other students have to say but the professors' responses to their comments and questions as well. The fact is, everything that goes on or is said in the room during class time is potentially important.

VIDEOS AND FILMS AREN'T A DAY OFF. When professors show films, DVDs, videos, or slides, or play audiotapes in class, they aren't doing so to entertain you. They are using them as part of the course material. You need to pay as close attention as when the professor is lecturing. Take notes on what is shown or played and consider the importance of it, just as you do when the professor is speaking.

THE END OF CLASS IS AS IMPORTANT AS THE BEGINNING. Don't click your pen, slam your book closed, and pack your backpack until the professor has indicated that class is over. It's not only rude, but information given at the end of class, even if it's given a few minutes after the class is supposed to officially end, may be the most useful. In college, professors determine when a class is over, not the clock, and certainly not you. And they often use the last few moments of each class to summarize major points, answer questions, and even offer hints about an upcoming exam.

So, although it may be tempting to tear out of the classroom when the class *should* be over and run off to your next class, lunch, conditioning, or practice, it's important to remain alert and attentive until the professor actually dismisses the class. What's more, if you have time before your next class, it's wise to spend a few minutes right after class (when what went on is still fresh in your mind) organizing your notes, highlighting key points, filling in missing information, and making notes in the margins. Of course, also make sure everything you've written is neat and legible so you'll be able to make sense of it when it comes time to study for exams. When possible, speak with the professor, teaching assistant, or a classmate to clarify anything you didn't fully understand or didn't completely get down in your notes.

> Some of the best notes I've ever taken have come after class when I jot down some things I remembered from a lecture after the fact. To maximize the benefits of your notes, try rewriting your notes each night to both review the material and prepare for your next class.
>
> — Audra Lissell

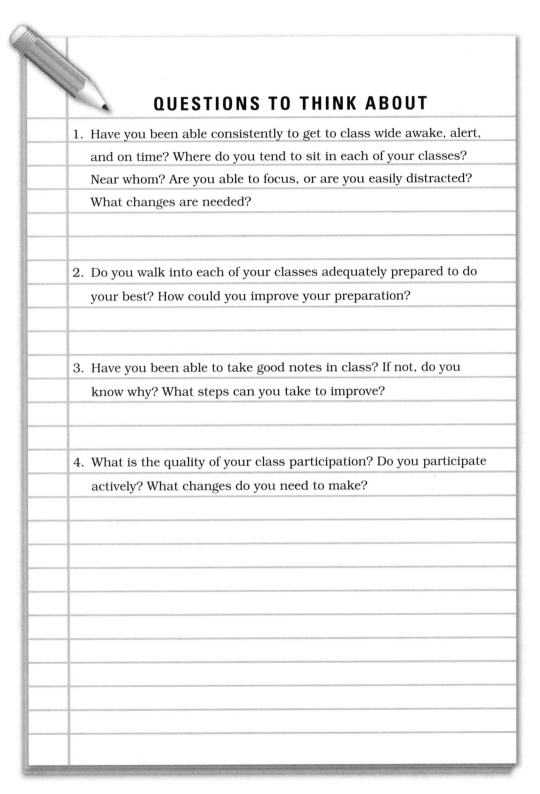

QUESTIONS TO THINK ABOUT

1. Have you been able consistently to get to class wide awake, alert, and on time? Where do you tend to sit in each of your classes? Near whom? Are you able to focus, or are you easily distracted? What changes are needed?

2. Do you walk into each of your classes adequately prepared to do your best? How could you improve your preparation?

3. Have you been able to take good notes in class? If not, do you know why? What steps can you take to improve?

4. What is the quality of your class participation? Do you participate actively? What changes do you need to make?

CHAPTER 8

Scoring Points with Faculty

> I tried to develop a positive relationship with my professors so they would
> like me as a person and respect me as a person.
>
> — Jon Larranaga

Before your first day of classes, you may not have any idea what college professors are like or how to deal with them. But you'll soon realize that they speak the same language you do, and they may listen to the same music, go to the same movies, eat pizza, and watch the same TV shows. They may even have an interest in your sport, may have participated in it, and might still participate on some level. That's because professors are regular people. They were once college students, too.

However, although they may be like you in many ways, there is one major difference: Your professors (sometimes aided by graduate students or teaching assistants) evaluate what you do. They're the ones who decide whether or not you pass your classes and what grades you receive. So you might think your professors and those who assist them are all-powerful or that your future is in their hands. But that's not the case. *Professors don't actually give grades; students earn them.* That means how well you do in a course is primarily in *your* hands.

How you relate to your professors and what they think of you can make a significant difference in how you do in your classes and how much you get out of your college experience. So when it comes to faculty, take advantage of every opportunity to score points by demonstrating you are a serious student who is as committed to academics as you are to athletics.

Tips from Peers and Profs

Establishing Productive Relationships with Faculty

PROFESSORS ARE HUMAN BEINGS. The stereotype of aloof, absentminded professors who are only interested in their esoteric research is rarely true. The vast majority of faculty members want to get to know their students, and they enjoy chatting with them about their subject as well as about matters of general interest.

BE MORE THAN JUST A NAME ON THE CLASS ROSTER. Get to know your professors and let them get to know you. The first part of that is pretty easy. After all, you only have four or five professors each semester. And it shouldn't be too tough to learn their names, including the correct spelling and pronunciation. On the other hand, your professors may have 150 or more students every semester, so it may take some effort to make yourself known to them. But it's worth it. Because once they get to know you and see that you are a serious student, professors are more likely to accommodate your special needs as an athlete. Take the initiative and introduce yourself to your professors early in the semester—if possible, right after the first or second class session.

Once your professors know who you are, meeting with them during office hours, using e-mail, or speaking on the telephone are the best ways to establish an ongoing relationship. But don't overdo it. Keep in mind that professors have their preferences, so get to know what they are and communicate using the method each one prefers. Also, remember that communicating with professors is different than with your friends and requires a different etiquette.

> Build a relationship with your professors. I don't mean sucking up. But profs can be great allies. When you're in a tough spot, they might help you out, give you the extension on that paper or let you take the test later. Besides, most professors are sports fans and understand that you are not a typical student.
>
> — Angela Whyte

> It's extremely important to meet your professors. During the first couple of weeks, go to office hours and introduce yourself. Most enjoy athletes and love to talk to you. If you don't do this, all they know you as is a number.
>
> — Spencer Harris

TIME-OUT!

Introduce yourself to each of your professors. Make an appointment to speak with at least one of them. Raise a point you found interesting or a question you had about a recent class. Discuss it in depth.

MAKE THE MOST OF CHANCE ENCOUNTERS. Unexpectedly running into a professor on or off campus and chatting can also be helpful in getting to know faculty. So if you notice one of your professors outside of class, don't pretend you don't see him or her. Take a moment and say hello. Be careful, however, because not all professors will respond well to greetings such as, "Yo! What up, Teach?" Use judgment in how you approach them and what you say. Remember, professors also have pulls on their time. So sometimes a brief "Hello" is enough.

USE FACULTY OFFICE HOURS. Virtually every professor is required to set aside a number of hours each week for the specific purpose of meeting with students. These hours are generally listed on the course syllabus or posted on the department bulletin board, Web page, or professor's office door. Unfortunately, many students fail to take advantage of these opportunities to meet one-on-one with their professors. Don't be one of those students! Make note of your professors' office hours, and use them.

You can usually just stop by to speak with your professors anytime during scheduled office hours. But to be on the safe side, it's a good idea to make an appointment. Also, although meetings in the professor's office are most common, some professors may prefer the faculty lounge or a local coffee shop. So make a note in your weekly planner when and where the meeting will take place. Think about what you want to discuss in advance. If you have specific questions or want to address certain issues, write them down and bring the list to your meeting.

Go to office hours even if you have a question you think is dumb. If professors see that you're making an effort to understand, they're more likely to help you out. Often, first-year courses are filled with hundreds of students and the professors hardly know anyone's name, so going into office hours puts a face to your name, and they will likely remember you when entering your final grade.

— Erin McIntyre

The majority of professors want students, especially student-athletes, to attend their office hours. This can be one of the best ways to shed the common misconception that athletes should be classified as poor students.

— Seth Neumuller

> ## TIME-OUT!
>
> List each of your professor's correctly spelled names, office location and phone number, e-mail address, and office hours. Make copies and put one on your bulletin board, another in your backpack, and still another in your travel bag. If you use a PDA, enter all the information into it.

Keeping Those Relationships

"PLEASE SEE ME." If a professor or teaching assistant has given you feedback on an assignment, consider what they mean and if you don't fully understand, ask for clarification. Then be sure to take their suggestions into account in future work, the same way you take advice from your coaches. And if the professor has written "Please see me" on something you handed in, be sure to do just that. Too many students don't follow through, fearing negatives. But professors view this as students just not caring.

ARRIVE ON TIME. If you're running late or need to cancel an appointment, have the courtesy to call the professor or department secretary as far in advance as possible, not at the last minute. You won't earn any points—and will probably lose a few—if you make an appointment and don't show up or arrive late and keep your professor waiting.

TALKING TO A PROFESSOR. In spite of their advanced degrees and in-depth knowledge, professors are just people. So don't be intimidated by the prospect of speaking with them. But remember, they have accomplished a great deal and deserve respect. Be friendly, inquisitive, and open to new learning. Listen to what they say, even if you disagree. Unless they indicate a preference, address faculty members as "doctor" or "professor," even if you aren't sure what their highest degree or academic rank is. If you are in academic difficulty or have gotten a test or paper back with comments you don't fully agree with or understand, show that you are committed to improving and are seeking the professor's guidance by being considerate and appreciative, not threatening, hostile, or aggressive. Don't try to hustle the professor or try to wrangle special favors simply because you are a varsity athlete. And don't make demands. Believe it or not, most professors want their students to do well in their courses and will try to be as helpful as they can—if you approach them appropriately.

FACULTY MEMBERS CAN BE VALUABLE ALLIES. Knowledge and new ideas are just part of what professors have to offer. They can also be an excellent source of career and graduate school information, provide employment leads and contacts, serve as references, and write letters of recommendation—but only if they have gotten to know you well enough. In addition, relationships you build with professors early in your college career can lead to opportunities to work closely and intensively with them in your junior and senior years. That kind of hands-on experience can be enormously rewarding and will look great on your résumé or graduate school application.

> Many universities have professors that have served in prestigious environments and in fields you are looking to pursue a career in. They are the masters of your interests. There's nothing better than having a person you can go to to discuss your academic future.
>
> — Audra Lissell
>
> My personal relationship with professors aided in my postgraduate career. I was able not only to get accurate and honest information about graduate school, but they went out of their way to help me in the grad school process. They took pride in assisting me in the application process by overseeing my writing sample, writing letters of recommendation, and helping narrow down my choices of schools.
>
> — Dan Bradley

PROFESSORS CAN BE DIFFICULT. Although you will find most faculty to be reasonable and accommodating, from time to time a problem might arise. For example, at the beginning of a semester when a professor learns you are a student-athlete, he or she might suggest that you drop the course by saying something like, "I don't care why or where your team is traveling, I don't permit absences." Or, having nothing to do with your being an athlete, a disagreement might arise over a grade or a point you make in a class discussion. Professors do make mistakes, and you have the right to review a grade or corrected material. So, no matter what the issue, if a problem arises, deal with it right away. Don't let it fester or grow, and don't blow it out of proportion. Your goal should be to turn a negative situation into a positive, not make it worse. As quickly as possible, make an appointment to speak with the professor. When you meet with him or her, remain calm and respectful. Don't go in with an attitude. If you can't reach a solution, discuss the situation with your Academic Advisor for Athletes or advisor in your major department. They will be in the best position to guide you or intervene on your behalf. But remember, the key is to address the problem promptly and appropriately, so that a solution can be reached and your academics won't be jeopardized.

POSITIVE RELATIONSHIPS CAN CONTINUE AFTER COURSES END. The end of a semester doesn't have to mean the end of the relationships you've established with your professors. When you have gotten to know a professor and value your relationship, keep in contact. An occasional e-mail, invitation to your team's competition, holiday greeting card, or just dropping by the professor's office for a quick "hello" will be appreciated. And remember, relationships can work in two directions: It's not only about professors helping you out. You may be able to assist them in a variety of significant ways.

Becoming good friends with some of my professors gave me an outlet away from sports. And I, in turn, have been able to help them in various ways. I have written recommendations when certain faculty were nominated for teaching awards; I have led discussions in classes they were not able to attend; I motivated them in their research; I filed proposals with the dean concerning the addition and change of specific courses; and I helped paint one's house. The bottom line is that I made many friends, not all of whom are fellow students.

— Dan Bradley

TIME-OUT!

Name one of your professors you think could become an academic mentor or role model for you. What about him or her do you admire? Why?

Absence Does *Not* Make Professor's Heart Grow Fonder

BE ABSENT WISELY. Just as anticipation is a key skill for most athletes, anticipation is critical when you are forced to miss class. As early in the semester as possible, notify your professors about classes you will have to miss because of competitions and travel. Ask your coach or Academic Advisor for Athletes to send notification to your professors listing the specific dates you will be absent. But don't assume everything will be taken care of just because you gave them a note. Professors have other concerns and may not remember, especially if you alerted them about your absences weeks in advance. So it's best to remind professors a few days before the classes you'll miss. And by all means, never ask a professor, "Am I going to miss anything?" Of course you're going to miss something! Be careful not to give the impression that you think what goes on in class is unimportant or a waste of time.

TALK TO PROFESSORS ABOUT THE SITUATION. Schedule appointments with professors to discuss your concerns about missing classes. Let them know you've made arrangements to get all the class notes from another student (or better yet, two). In addition, consider asking the professors' permission to have a classmate tape lectures and class discussions while you are gone. Also, ask professors if they could give you assignments and handouts ahead of time, and offer to submit work in advance of due dates rather than requesting extensions.

If you will be forced to miss an examination, ask the professor if he or she would prefer that you take the exam earlier than the rest of the class or when you return to campus. Or suggest the possibility of submitting an alternative assignment or having the exam proctored while your team is on the road. Stay in touch with the professor or classmates while you're on the road. E-mail is great for this. If you demonstrate that you are a serious, responsible student, most professors will accommodate your special needs as a student-athlete. But in the unlikely event that a solution cannot be found, immediately bring this to the attention of your Academic Advisor for Athletes.

> As an athlete, you are bound to miss classes. This may appear to be a treat at first, but in the long run it can hurt your chances of a good grade. If you know you are going to miss a class, talk to the professor. Most professors are understanding about your other commitments and will tell you to get the notes from someone else, or they will give you an assignment to do beforehand so you aren't playing catch-up later on. Showing your professors that you plan ahead exhibits a desire to succeed.
>
> — Audra Lissell

NOT ALL ABSENCES CAN BE ANTICIPATED. No matter how carefully you plan ahead, unforeseen things like canceled flights, buses that break down, injuries, family emergencies, or serious illness can keep you from attending class. If you have to miss class for any reason other than athletic scheduling conflicts (which you were aware of and planned for in advance), try to notify your professor by leaving a telephone or e-mail message, or contact the professor's secretary. Again, you want to demonstrate that you regret having to miss class and provide assurances that you will catch up as soon as possible. Because unexpected things do come up, it's essential that as early in the semester as possible you get the phone numbers and e-mail addresses of at least two students in each of your courses. Be selective: Choose classmates who are reliable and take comprehensive notes, not just friends who may pay little attention in class. If you miss class, contact a classmate and make arrangements to copy the class notes, get all the handouts, and find out about all the assignments so you can complete them as quickly as possible to avoid falling behind.

EXCUSES, EXCUSES. Forget about trying to scam your professors. They've heard all the excuses before. "We were on a road trip and got back to campus too late," "I left the paper in the hotel," "My computer crashed," "The printer ran out of ink," "I had to see the team physician to . . ." These won't work! In the past, students missed classes because they came down with a virus; now, assignments aren't handed in because the computer came down with one. The dog used to eat term papers; these days, computers are eating disks. Face up to your responsibilities! If you aren't prepared to hand in an assignment on time, have to be late to class, or miss class entirely, make an appointment and explain to your professor what's going on. And tell the truth. If you demonstrate you care about your studies and their courses, most professors will understand, as long as these situations don't arise too often.

QUESTIONS TO THINK ABOUT

1. Have you made your professors aware that you are a student-athlete? What were their reactions?

2. What steps have you taken to develop positive relationships with your professors? What have been the results?

3. Do you have a professor who seems hostile to having athletes in his or her class? What have you done to deal with the situation? Is there anything else you could or should do?

4. Have you invited any of your professors to a game or competition? Have you even thought about it? Why not?

CHAPTER 9

Learning to Study and Studying to Learn

My goal in college was to do my best. I was taught that some people might be more gifted or talented, *but* no one should ever outhustle or outwork me.

— Abraham Billy Hardee III

Ask student-athletes (or any students, for that matter) about studying, and virtually all will tell you it's not high on their list of favorite activities. Faced with a jam-packed schedule, the reality is that spending time studying means forgoing things you'd much rather be doing. Given a choice between hanging out with friends, watching TV, playing video games, taking a nap, talking on the phone, or studying, it's no contest: Studying loses, hands down.

But let's think about studying a different way. When you compete as an athlete, your goal is to perform to the best of your abilities. And you know that being prepared is key. Going into competition without adequate conditioning, practice, and preparation is asking for trouble. The same holds true when it comes to earning good grades in your courses. Studying is the preparation you need to perform your best in the competitive environment of the classroom. It's how you prepare not only to meet the requirements of your courses and earn good grades but to turn in the kind of academic performance that meets your personal standards *and* to learn. And much like the preparation necessary to excel at your sport, studying requires more than minimum time and effort, unless you want merely to squeak by academically.

We don't think you're the kind of person who is satisfied with barely getting by. If you were, you wouldn't be competing at the college level. But just as being a member of a college team probably requires more rigorous and thorough preparation than in high school, succeeding academically in college requires a different kind of studying than you've had to do in the past.

This chapter is designed to get you thinking about your study mind-set and about ways of enhancing your study skills and strategies. It provides a range of ideas for you to consider, try out, and evaluate. We hope you'll find methods and strategies that will work for you.

Keep in mind, however, that no matter what method or strategy works best for you, studying always begins in the classroom. If you're following the advice offered in the preceding two chapters, you're getting to class on time, attending regularly, staying focused, taking useful notes, and participating appropriately in class discussions. By doing this, you're already laying a solid foundation that will help you study.

One more thing: Developing good study habits early in your college years will benefit you long after you've graduated. The skills, strategies, and habits you develop and use today will serve you well in graduate or professional school and in whatever career you pursue.

Tips from Peers and Profs

Why Study? Defining Academic Success

WHAT DOES ACADEMIC SUCCESS MEAN? Coaches or teammates might refer to the NCAA Manual and tell you that academic success means "maintaining satisfactory progress toward degree requirements." The academic authorities at your college along with the conference in which your school competes determine the number of credits or credit hours student-athletes are required to "satisfactorily complete" each semester or quarter if they are to be eligible to compete. In addition, to be considered academically successful as a student-athlete, you have to maintain the minimum GPA that allows you to be "in good academic standing." Accomplish these, and you're academically eligible to compete. Of course, you want to know what these minimum standards are. But as an athlete, you know that to be successful you have to do a lot better than meet minimum standards. And that certainly holds true when it comes to academics.

TIME-OUT!

At your school, what is the minimum number of credit hours that student-athletes are required to complete each semester or quarter? The minimum GPA you need to maintain? List three reasons why just meeting these minimums isn't good enough for you.

YOUR PROFS HAVE THEIR OWN DEFINITIONS OF ACADEMIC SUCCESS. In chapter 7 you learned about how a course syllabus can be thought of as your road map to an *A*. Each professor has his or her own course objectives and expectations for what a student must accomplish to earn an *A*, a *B*, and so on. The syllabus most likely itemizes, with weighted percentages, how exams, written assignments, class participation, and other criteria contribute to your final course grade. Be sure you know how final grades will be determined for each of your classes.

ONLY *YOU* CAN DEFINE TRUE LEARNING. Too often, students confuse getting passing grades with learning. They memorize the required material for exams, but the moment the semester ends, they forget much of it. Whatever they supposedly learned vaporizes. Even though they might have gotten a good grade in the class, they haven't really learned much of anything. True learning is about more than earning passing (or even good) grades in your courses. It's about retaining or holding on to the ideas, ways of thinking, and information presented in your classes long after you leave college. It's about integrating the material into your own thought processes and applying it as you go through life. So ultimately, true learning is about personal growth, about making what you are exposed to in the classroom part of who you are and who you will become.

TIME-OUT!

Think back to high school. List five important ideas (not simple facts) that you learned and still remember. Why have these ideas remained with you?

GRADES CERTAINLY ARE ALSO IMPORTANT. You're sure to hear students talking about their 3.2's and 2.3's. Ideally, when you talk about your GPA, it will be high. On most college campuses, how well or how poorly you're doing academically is reflected by the computation of your GPA. Each letter grade is assigned a numerical value (e.g., A = 4, B = 3, C = 2), and at the end of every semester or quarter, you'll earn the term's GPA based on the average of the number values of the letter grades you receive in your courses and the number of credits each course is assigned. You'll also have a cumulative GPA ("cume") that is based on the grades you received for all the courses you've taken at the school. Your school might also compute the cume earned in your major. Not all colleges grade the same way, though. So check your college's catalog or bulletin for specific information about grades, GPAs, and methods of calculation.

Although grades aren't necessarily a reflection of what you've learned, they do mean a lot. Beyond needing to maintain the minimum GPA required to compete or keep your scholarship, it's likely that your grades will matter when you apply for a summer job or internship. And certainly when you seek full-time employment or admission to graduate or professional school, your GPA will weigh heavily. A high GPA may also qualify you for a variety of academic honors and grants. So always strive to get the highest grades you can.

Maintain a Positive Academic Mind-Set

BE PROUD OF DOING WELL IN CLASS. In chapter 2 we said being an athlete doesn't mean you have to be antiintellectual or antiacademic. But it's easy to fall into that trap. Many student-athletes tend to receive far greater recognition and reinforcement for their athletic performance than for their academic accomplishments. On some campuses, especially where athletes are housed together in a separate dorm and isolated from the general student body, student-athletes who are academically focused may even be ridiculed and discouraged by other athletes. But think about it: You have the opportunity to benefit from a valuable college education, possibly with a scholarship or other form of financial aid. Why not take full advantage of the opportunity? View yourself as the intelligent person you are. There's absolutely no need to be ashamed of it.

JUMP OFF TO A GOOD START. Too many college athletes are so focused on doing well in their sport when they first arrive on campus that academics takes a backseat. In fact, many go through their first 2 years so athletically driven that they don't begin to pay close attention to their studies until their junior year. So be careful, because once you've taken a lot of courses and earned many credits, it's harder to raise your GPA. Chances are you don't want to fall behind in a competition and have to play catch-up, and it's the same with grades. Dedicate yourself to getting off to the best possible academic start at the beginning of each semester, right from your first semester, and stay as far out in front academically as you can.

> Work hard your first semester because it's much easier to keep up a good GPA rather than trying to build one up after messing around your first semester. Some of my teammates are still trying to recover from their freshman year, and they're seniors now.
>
> — Erin McIntyre
>
> Get off to a great start. It's very important to get your college career started on a high note. Not only does this prove to yourself that you belong, but it also shows your professors, coaches, and teammates that you're serious about your education.
>
> — Jon Larranaga

DON'T SETTLE FOR JUST PASSING. As an athlete, you're used to setting goals and focusing on achieving them in a disciplined way. Having a goal provides focus, helps maintain dedication and commitment, and gives you a target to shoot for. Challenging, yet realistic, goals lead to working harder and achieving more. It's the same for academic goal setting. You don't want to set academic goals that you can't possibly reach, but you also don't want to set goals that are too easy. If you do, you'll only shortchange yourself. As an athlete, your goal hasn't been to be just average. And it shouldn't be your goal as a student either. Shoot for the A's and B's. Forget the C's.

> You have to make your sport *and* your grades priorities.
>
> — Shelbylynn McBride

BOUNCE BACK WHEN YOU'RE DOWN. At some point in college you're likely to find yourself in a course or two that, no matter how hard you work and how much you study, you just can't seem to do well. Just about every student has that experience. You've probably been in that kind of situation in your sport. You or your team is way behind. You need to step up and show what you're made of! The same applies to academics. Blaming your poor performance on lousy professors, boring courses, or lack of sleep or study time is a cop-out. As an athlete, you know the importance of ditching the excuses and of *taking responsibility*. And you've learned to bounce back, to demonstrate resilience. Now as a college student, when you need to, reach deep inside yourself and apply that same attribute to your academics.

> Never give up, even when things get rough. If you push through the difficult times you will come out thankful for the experience and, most importantly, appreciate the education.
>
> — Jennifer Johnstone

STAY POSITIVE! Talk to yourself: "I can do this! I will do this!"

> School work is mental. You must incorporate self-suggestion in all aspects of life. When I am on the court I always say mentally, "Mo, you are the best player on the court; show everyone what you are made of."
>
> — Maurice Yearwood

Academic "Have To's"

YES, YOU DO HAVE TO BUY YOUR OWN BOOKS. Some students think they can "get over" by not purchasing required books. But this idea usually backfires. Sharing books with classmates or copying pages from someone else's texts are recipes for disaster. You also can't count on borrowing course books from the library. Other students may get them before you do, and even if the books are available, you may not be allowed to take them out of the building, and you can't mark them. So you *must* have your own books. It's the only way to be sure they'll be available when you need them. And you'll be able to mark them, highlight, underline, and make notes in the margins to help you study.

But to be on the safe side, don't put any marks in a new text until you're certain you'll be staying in the class and it is, in fact, the book the professor wants you to use. As with everything you buy, always keep receipts and be familiar with the store's refund policy. Once you know you'll be using the books, be sure to put your name and a contact number or e-mail address on the inside cover in case they get misplaced or lost. After the course is over, don't sell a book unless you are absolutely sure you won't need it again in a follow-up course. And don't sell books in your major. Keep them and begin to build your own academic library for use in advanced courses and your future profession.

USED BOOKS ARE AN OPTION. Textbooks can be ridiculously expensive. So if your scholarship doesn't fully cover their cost, you may want to consider buying used copies with a lower price tag. But be careful. Make sure you get the correct edition, and look for used books that aren't too marked up with another student's thoughts. Don't ever rely on another student's highlighting or margin notes. He or she may have done poorly in the course.

BACKPACKS WITHOUT BOOKS? Another way to potentially save money is with e-textbooks. Customized, interactive digital textbooks and electronic versions of printed textbooks are increasingly appearing on campus bookstore shelves. Among the advantages are that they cost less, weigh less, take up less space than their printed versions, and can be downloaded onto your laptop or PDA. They allow the user to make margin notes and highlight text, and can be used with programs that read the text aloud, enabling students to do their reading while conditioning or standing on line at the convenience store. But be careful! To prevent students from copying and sharing these books, some e-textbooks have 6-month or 1-year expiration dates, and publishers have set limits on the number of pages that can be printed each week, thereby limiting the amount of reading you can do. Another downside for students pressed for cash at the end of the semester is that e-textbooks can't be resold.

YOU HAVE TO DO YOUR HOMEWORK. Even though the assignments you get might not be called homework and may never be collected by your professors, *do them!* Whether they're readings listed in a course syllabus or assignments distributed in class, believe it or not, your professors aren't giving you busywork. The assignments may be designed to stimulate critical thinking, the material may appear on exams, and future course work may be based on work you've been asked to complete outside of class. Be sure you understand and follow your professor's instructions. Do what the instructor wants you to do, the way he or she wants it done. Each professor has a personal way of doing things, and you have to respect it.

MEET ALL DEADLINES. When you are expected to come to class having read specific pages, be sure you've read them before class. If you've been asked to prepare a presentation for an upcoming class session, have it done for that session. And if a written assignment is due at the beginning of class on a specific date, turn it in at the beginning of class on that day. Remember, student-athletes have to follow the same rules and are held to the same standards as other students. Athletics-related explanations, like team travel or extra practice, do not automatically excuse late or incomplete assignments or lack of preparation for class. If you have a legitimate reason for not being prepared, make sure you contact the professor as far ahead of time as possible, explain the situation, and ask what you need to do. And make sure it doesn't happen too often!

TIME-OUT!

For each course you are currently taking, list the homework that's been assigned for next week. How long do you anticipate each assignment will take to complete? When will you begin working on the assignments?

DEMONSTRATE CARE IN THE WORK YOU SUBMIT. It isn't enough to meet deadlines if the work you hand in is sloppy and full of typographical and grammatical errors. Nor is it an acceptable excuse that you just came from practice and there was mud in your gym bag that got on your work or your file folder got crushed in your locker. Allowing any of these to happen gives your professors the message that you really don't care—about them or their courses. The work you submit is seen as a reflection of who you are and how much you care about your courses. So be sure to proofread your writing carefully and make all necessary corrections. Don't count on spell check or grammar check to do a complete job of picking up mistakes. They aren't always reliable. So it's also a good idea to ask a friend or teammate who has a critical eye to look over your assignments before submitting them. And if proofreading is an area you're weak in, ask your Academic Advisor for Athletes where you can get help.

TAKE YOUR PROFESSORS' COMMENTS SERIOUSLY. Whether you are satisfied with your grade or not, when your work is returned to you, don't wad it in a ball and toss it in the trash or file it away never to be looked at again. Carefully review professors' comments, corrections, and suggestions. Your work, and what your professors say about it, will often prove helpful in preparing future assignments and studying for future exams.

USE COMPUTERS FOR MORE THAN E-MAILING FRIENDS. In college you must know how to use the computer to prepare course assignments and write papers; communicate with professors, coaches, and fellow students; retrieve information from the library and various databases; and access course and faculty Web sites. You may even register for classes, take exams, and submit homework online. So given the severe time pressures that you face, life will probably be a lot easier if you have access to a laptop or desktop computer 24/7. If you don't own one, be sure you know of at least two convenient locations on campus where, and during what hours, computers and printers are available. If you are fortunate enough to own a laptop—or if your Athletics Department makes loaners available—make it a habit to take it along when traveling. And use it to play games, download music, or watch DVDs only *after* you've used it to complete your academic assignments.

> I always bring books and my laptop to away games. There are several hours on the bus and in hotel rooms that are useful for studying.
>
> — Shelbylynn McBride

BACK UP YOUR WORK. Most campuses specify the preferred hardware (PC or Mac) and software for word processing or other purposes. Know what they are and how to use them. You also *must* get into the habit of backing up all your work, not just on the computer's hard drive, but on a disk, CD, or flash or jump drive as well. And it's smart to print out an additional hard copy. No matter how expert you are, computer glitches and printer malfunctions can, and will, occur, usually at the worst possible time. So a word to the wise: Get your work done early enough so that if a problem arises, you have time to resolve or work around it.

LEARN AND FOLLOW CAMPUS COMPUTER ETIQUETTE. This is especially important when dealing with professors. For example, don't submit assignments electronically or on a disk unless you're certain the professor will accept them that way. You might be in for a horrible surprise if you assume he or she will accept work sent electronically or handed in on a disk because many professors won't. Also, remember that professors aren't your buddies. Unless you've cleared it with them beforehand, keep them off your "Buddy List." And one final word: If your e-mail or screen name is anything like "bigbat69" or "sexymamaDD," consider getting rid of it. Your professors and many fellow students might not appreciate or see the humor in it.

The Fundamentals of Studying

WHY DO *YOU* STUDY? There's a big difference between studying because you want to learn and studying just because you're going to be tested. The more you want to learn what you study, the easier it will be to absorb the material and the more likely you'll remember it when you're facing an exam and after the exam is over. So when you sit down to study, don't think in terms of having to take a test. Try to establish a good reason or set of reasons for you to learn what you are studying. Then think about and get a handle on the big ideas first. That's where you'll usually find the best reasons to learn material. Once you have a grasp of the big ideas, it's far easier to commit the specifics and details to memory and more likely you'll do well when you are tested. The better able you are to see course material as connected to your life, the easier it will be to learn and the less time and effort you'll have to put into studying it.

SET SPECIFIC LONG-TERM AND SHORT-TERM GOALS. Chances are that setting goals is nothing new for you. You do it all the time to help you perform better in competition. Academically, you've got to do the same. For example, a semester goal might be to complete the required English composition course with a grade of B or better; a weekly goal might be to submit all writing assignments on time; and a daily goal could be to spend at least an hour each day freewriting in your journal. Other short-term goals might relate to meeting regularly with a tutor or spending at least 2 hours each day or evening studying. Write out a daily or weekly study checklist and stick to it. Also, keep a record of accomplishments. You've probably done this in your sport—listing your best times or foul shooting percentages, for example. In addition, you may want to establish a written contract with your academic advisor outlining specific goals and schedule weekly meetings to monitor your progress. That way you'll build a sense of academic discipline enforced both internally and externally.

TIME-OUT!

Select one course you are taking this semester. What is your long-term goal in the course? List three short-term goals that will help you accomplish it.

VERY SHORT-TERM GOALS CAN ALSO BE HELPFUL. Depending on your level of academic endurance (how long you're able to stay focused at one sitting), you may find it beneficial to break up an assignment or a time period into smaller segments. For example, "I'll read 15 pages of the assignment and make margin notes, and then I'll take a shower. After that I'll come back and read the next 15 pages." "I'll work on the math assignment for 40 minutes and then I'll call home. Then I'll put in another 40 minutes." This is a helpful strategy because you're not only breaking up your studying into more manageable pieces, you're also rewarding yourself when you complete each segment of the task. Enjoy those rewards, and then return to studying followed by another reward. Before you know it, you'll accomplish one or more of your longer-term goals.

> Especially freshman year, try to make study periods moderately sized (an hour or two at most) because if they're too long, you'll fool yourself into thinking you have an endless amount of time.
>
> — Mariko Tansey Holbrook

> When studying for long periods of time I take deliberate breaks. When it comes to studying at night, I found good results with doing something active, like push-ups and sit-ups. This gives me the break I need and the blood flow and energy to keep concentrating.
>
> — Tim Donnelly

BE GENEROUS WITH THE REWARDS YOU GIVE YOURSELF. We're not only talking about a shower or a phone call. The more challenging the task, the more fun the reward ought to be. Do your math problem sets, and then go out and throw a Frisbee with friends for a while. Complete the term paper that's been hanging over your head, and then treat yourself to a movie. Rewards like these are useful motivators, especially when you need an extra push or incentive to get your work done.

WHERE SHOULD YOU STUDY? Where you study and the conditions in that environment have a lot to do with how successful you will be at getting your work done. The right place to study is the one that works best for *you*. Generally speaking, it's best to find a spot that has good lighting and ventilation, is free of distractions, and is comfortable but not too comfortable. And of course, the environment must accommodate whatever it is you need to do: for example, read, write, use a computer, consult references, or spread out maps, books, and materials. Beyond these basics, it's really a matter of personal preference.

Students have been able to study successfully almost anywhere, from traditional locations (the library, a desk or bed, residence study lounge, vacant classroom, under a tree) to less traditional spots (the bathtub, a chapel pew, car, local café). And student-athletes also have additional possibilities like a vacant gym or playing field, conditioning room, study hall, on a bus or plane, in a terminal waiting area, or hotel room.

> I prefer studying in an environment conducive to learning. I surround myself with nonathletes who are constantly work oriented. When I see them putting in study hours and working hard, it drives me to join them in tough times — for example, after practice when I feel inclined to relax.
>
> — Dan Blankenship

> Many times I forced myself to go to the library because I knew that if I sat in my room and tried to get work done, I'd be easily distracted by visitors, phones, food, and noise. For me, the dorm is not a good place to study.
>
> — Johanna DiChiara-Drab

WHAT ABOUT STUDY HALL? It's likely that your coach will require you to attend mandatory study hall both on campus and on the road. Although this can be useful in forcing you to budget time to hit the books, there's a problem: Being around teammates can be distracting. It may be difficult, but rather than waste the time socializing, focus on why you're there—to study—and do just that.

> Coaches usually require athletes to study in study hall, but I find study hall is more of a social environment than a study environment.
>
> — Shelbylynn McBride

TV OR RADIO ON OR OFF? Are you better off with or without music? What type of music? TV on, off, or muted? Roommates present or not around? Study partners or solo? While eating or munching or snack free? Earplugs? Earbuds? Caffeinated or decaf? These are decisions you have to make consciously, and no absolutes apply to everyone. Some students have been known purposely to study where they are likely to be distracted, or they create distractions for themselves to minimize the pain of studying. You have to think honestly about what you want to get out of studying and what works best to make it possible. Then do some experimenting with locations and conditions, and stick with what works.

> Once you have identified your particular distractions, make an effort to avoid them. If the constant noise of people walking around is a distraction, then the library may be a good place. If, however, you find complete quiet a distraction (like I sometimes do), maybe you should try working alone in your room with soft music playing.
>
> — Brandi Cross

WHEN TO STUDY. It's not enough to just think about *where* to study. You have to also consider *when*. In chapters 4 and 5 we discussed time management, scheduling, and all of the time commitments you have pulling on you as a student-athlete. So ask yourself some important questions such as these: What times of the day am I most awake and alert (morning or night person)? When do I have the highest energy level? When are fun things *not* happening on campus (you probably don't want to spend 6 hours in the library on the Saturday of Homecoming Weekend)?

> After a long day of classes and practice, I'm often tired. I lose my attention span at this point. As a result, I often get my best studying done in the morning. I tend to read at night and do my memorization in the morning.
>
> — Patricia Metzger

> It depends what works best for you, but I've found afternoons in the library before practice are usually my most productive times.
>
> — Mariko Tansey Holbrook

> People tend to think that the weekends are time to relax, but I like to get a lot of work done on Sundays, especially in the morning when everyone is still sleeping from staying out late on Saturday night.
>
> — Erin McIntyre

TIME-OUT!

List the conditions you find optimal for studying (location, time of day, etc.). Speak with two academically successful teammates about the conditions they prefer when studying. Compare your list with theirs.

ON THE ROAD AGAIN. It's not just a Willie Nelson tune. In figuring out the where and when of studying, you also have to take account of all the days when your team is traveling. We discussed this in chapter 4, but it's worth reiterating. Although you probably won't be able to do any serious academic work close to competition, event, or game time, on most road trips there is lots of downtime when there's nothing going on and not much to do. Getting work done during these times will make otherwise boring times pass more quickly. So whether you're on a bus, plane, or train or in a terminal or hotel room, don't wait for mandatory study hours to be announced. Take advantage of the free time, find a place that works for you, and get some work done. When you return to campus, you'll be glad you did.

> I am on the road a lot, and it can be very difficult to study on the bus with teammates hanging out, talking, or watching movies. One strategy I have learned when I desperately need to study for a test or read a chapter is to block out all the noise by putting on my headphones and playing a certain beat. This beat helps keep the rest of the noise out while still allowing me to concentrate on what I am reading.
>
> — Julie Ruff

HOW MUCH TIME? You may have heard the formula, "2 hours of study for every hour of class." In other words, if you're enrolled for 15 credits or class hours each week, you should plan on spending about 30 hours a week hitting the books. This includes reading, completing assignments, studying for exams, and doing library research. Of course, this is just an average, a guide. Some weeks you may need to put in more time; other weeks less. There is no exact formula for academic success that works for everyone. Some students need to devote more time; others do well with less. And don't forget, some schools, courses, and professors are more demanding than others. So you have to understand your own abilities, evaluate the academic demands placed on you, and put in as much time as necessary for you to succeed.

RESULTS MATTER, NOT THE NUMBER OF HOURS YOU PUT IN. Be careful not to think just in terms of how long you study because your professors don't really care how many hours you put in. They care about the grades you get on exams and the quality of the papers you submit. Think about it: In your sport you know when you just go through the motions at practice. No matter how long the practice was, chances are it won't be helpful when it comes time to compete. Similarly, merely going through the motions of sitting at a desk with a book open and pen in hand doesn't mean you're studying effectively. You can sit for 60 hours a week under perfect study conditions, but if you don't retain anything, you've wasted your time. The key is how well you really are using the precious out-of-class time you put aside for studying. So as you study, test yourself periodically to make sure you're focused and actually retaining the material.

What's important is the quality of your efforts and the results you achieve, not the number of hours you're devoting. If you're completing assignments, earning high grades, and the learning is staying with you, you're making good use of your study time. If, however, you aren't satisfied with the results of your efforts, go back to the drawing board and try some different approaches.

ALONE OR WITH OTHERS? Some students feel they learn better when they study by themselves. They don't have to compromise with anyone or feel extra pressures about time, place, or amount of preparation. Nor are they bothered by the distractions of having other people around. They set their own pace and move through the material however they wish. And they don't have to worry about their overly anxious study mates making them more nervous than they already are. Other students find they learn better when they study with a partner or as a member of a small study group (five or fewer participants is a good size). Classmates can help each other prepare, review, stay focused, provide an extra dose of motivation, and offer support when someone is having difficulty. When everyone holds up their end, the group can accomplish a lot, and meetings can be extremely productive. But without ground rules and a serious commitment by all the members, meetings can be a total waste of time as members chat, joke around, eat and drink, or spend too much time complaining about the course or professor.

> Do not study with fellow athletes. That will always lend itself to procrastination and poor time management. You will find yourself talking about your last game rather than physics.
>
> — Jason Roberts

> I suggest studying with people early in the review process but not right before the exam. Get a feeling for what everyone else is thinking, and then apply that to your own personal study time. You don't want your last hours before the exam to be spent explaining something you understand to someone who really doesn't have a clue.
>
> — Audra Lissell

> Don't call the girl you like over to study with you. Nothing will get done. Call her *after* you study!
>
> — Nate Jones

Getting the Most from Your Readings

IT BEGINS WITH YOUR APPROACH TO THE MATERIAL. When you sit down to work with assigned readings, what is your goal? Your professor had a goal in mind when he or she assigned the material, and you need to have a goal in mind when you read it. But if your goal is *just* to spend a specified amount of time with a chapter, or *just* to get through a predetermined number of pages, chances are you aren't going to get much out of it. The goal must be to digest the material so you understand it, it means something to you, and the understanding and meaning stay with you when you go to class, take exams, and, most importantly, when you want to use it in your life outside of the classroom.

It's similar to the way you might approach strengthening a specific athletic skill. For example, if you're a basketball player with a weak foul shot, you might hit the gym 3 days a week and shoot 100 foul shots each time. Your goal is not to put in extra practice time. It's to improve your shooting so that when you're in a game you'll do a better job of sinking your shots. Apply the same attitude to working with your course readings. Read with a goal in mind. Read with a purpose. And no matter what, always read assigned materials *before* they are lectured about or discussed in class. Then, after class, read them again.

> Read the required course materials. There is probably a reason it was assigned. That way, you are at least familiar with all of the topics being covered. Now studying simply becomes a review of the material you have already seen, and you already have good notes and a highlighted book from which to study.
>
> — Jim Olds

DIFFERENT READING MATERIALS REQUIRE DIFFERENT APPROACHES. Depending on the courses you take, you'll be assigned a variety of different types of readings. Among these will be essays, novels, plays, poetry, newspaper and magazine articles, professional journal articles, case studies, and textbooks. Textbooks are usually not fun! But much of your reading will be in textbooks, especially in your first and second years at college. Textbooks are designed to provide students with broad, basic information, and lots of it. The material probably won't grab, engage, or entertain you. So when you find yourself spacing out or losing focus when reading a textbook (or any of your assigned readings), the onus is on you to catch yourself, refocus, and engage the readings as best you can. This may not be easy, but what follows are some suggestions that can be effective.

APPROACH ASSIGNMENTS WITH A PLAN AND TAKE CONTROL OF YOUR READING. Begin by addressing some basic questions: Why did the professor assign this reading? What is the author's underlying purpose (e.g., to provide information, offer an opinion)? How has the author organized the information (e.g., in order of importance, historical significance, or contrasting points of view)? What appears to be most relevant, least important, and why? How does the reading relate to classroom lectures, the professor's personal interest, and the anticipated emphasis of upcoming exams? In what ways does the reading connect with what you already know? By addressing these kinds of questions, you will be engaging the material and be more likely to get something out of it.

BE ACTIVE WITH THE READINGS. There are quite a few systematic reading and studying methods that successful students believe in and have found very helpful. One or more of these systems probably are taught on your campus, most likely through the Learning Center or Office of Academic Enhancement (see chapter 3). No matter what the methods are called, they are quite similar, and they all follow a series of sequenced steps that push students to actively engage the material. You may have learned one or more of these in high school. Among the methods are PMTC, PQR3, PQRST, SOAR, MUDDER, and even MURDER.

THE METHOD MOST COMMONLY USED IS SQ3R. Developed by Professor Francis Robinson at Ohio State University (1970), SQ3R helps make reading more meaningful by encouraging students to use these steps:

1. **Survey.** Before beginning to read material, do a quick overview of the chapter's headings, subheadings, boldfaced or italicized terms, introduction, summary, and charts and graphs.
2. **Question.** Based on the initial overview of the chapter, develop questions you may have about the material. You can also include questions that the author might have provided at the beginning or end of the chapter.
3. **Read.** Read each section of the chapter, seeking answers to the questions you posed. Pay special attention to the main ideas and supporting details. When you find the answer, reflect on the meaning of the material as you answer your questions. Mark your book, underline, bracket, highlight, and make notes in the margins. The key is going beyond merely reading to becoming as active as necessary to learn the material.
4. **Recite.** Think about what you have just learned. As you move through each section of the chapter, in your own words say out loud (yes, out

loud) or write down a summary of the main ideas along with the answers to the earlier questions.

5. **Review.** After completing steps 1 through 4, try to review the most important points you remember. You can do this after you've finished reading and before an exam. Don't be shy about seeking clarification or explanation from your professor or classmates. They will respect you for being truly interested in learning the material.

MARK YOUR TEXTS FREELY. Remember, in college you own your books, so you can do whatever you wish to them. Fold the pages, underline or highlight key passages or terms, write notes to yourself in the margins, use asterisks, checks, stars, happy faces, or whatever else you want to call attention to key spots in the reading. But be selective. If you underline or highlight everything, it won't be very helpful or efficient when you have to study the material. By being active and thoughtful with your marking, you're more likely to remember the material, and you'll be able to find and return easily to those important points should you need to at a later date.

NOTE TAKING ISN'T JUST FOR LECTURES. Although many students find it useful to mark their books, others find it an even better study technique to take careful notes on the reading using a dedicated notebook or separate sheets of paper. The advantage is that when it's time to study for an exam, they don't have to go page by page through a thick text. They just use their notes and refer back to the book only for clarification.

DON'T FORGET THE INDEX CARDS. Along with SQ3R or whatever other study method they may be using, many successful students study from 3 by 5 index cards. For example, you may write a topic, key idea, or question on one side of the card and the full explanation on the flip side. The advantage of using index cards is that because they're small, the cards are convenient to pull out at any time and can be used for any length of time, even 5- to 10-minute periods before class or mealtime. Also, their small size forces you to summarize the most important information in your own words. In addition, you can integrate reading and class notes on the cards. As you study the information for an exam, you can easily separate out what you've mastered from what you still need to work on.

QUESTIONS TO THINK ABOUT

1. What does being academically successful mean to you? What strategies have you developed to achieve it? Are you employing those strategies?

2. If you're not as academically successful as you'd like, what can you do to improve your performance? When will you begin?

3. Where is the best place for you to study? How long can you stay focused when studying there? What is the best time of day for you to maximize the efforts you put into studying?

4. How do you judge if you're studying effectively or just going through the motions? Do you engage the material actively or leaf through it passively? What changes do you think you ought to make?

CHAPTER 10

Delivering at Crunch Time

Doing Your Best on Exams

> Contrary to most students' wishes, there is no magic formula for succeeding on tests. Rather, the only way to ensure that you will do well is by knowing the material. The best way to prepare for exams is by going to class, paying attention, and reading the book(s).
>
> — Jim Olds

You may be only a freshman, but chances are you've already taken and done well on more tests than most students on campus. After all, you're a varsity athlete, and every competition you've ever been in was actually a test of what your coaches taught and how much of it you learned. And you've demonstrated that you know how to face those tests and achieve excellent results. You've mastered the formula for athletic success: Pay careful attention to what your coaches say, train diligently, focus on the task at hand, and apply your skills during competition. Following the same formula will go a long way to ensuring that you succeed on tests in your academic courses as well: Pay careful attention to what your professors say, study diligently, focus on the task at hand, and apply your academic skills during exams.

Chapters 7, 8, and 9 discussed how you can build a solid foundation, so that at crunch time—exam day—you're able to step up and deliver. Ideally, you have already begun to master skills like understanding and recalling most of the important information from lectures, discussions, and readings, and you're making the necessary connections with your own thinking about the material. In addition, if you're having difficulty doing any of these, you're not letting pride get in the way. You're getting the assistance you need.

Now it's time to focus on some of the actual nuts and bolts of pregame preparation, managing the exam itself, and following up after the exam has been graded (so you'll be able to do even better on the next one). Unfortunately, just as there's no magic that can guarantee you will win every athletic competition, there's no magic that'll guarantee you ace all your exams. But in this chapter you'll find insights and tips that can help you earn the kind of grades you are capable of achieving.

Tips from Peers and Profs

Success Begins with Meaningful Preparation

PREPARE WELL, AND YOU'RE MORE LIKELY TO PERFORM WELL. As an athlete, you know how important preparation is. If you haven't prepared adequately, your coach might not permit you to compete. And even if you are allowed to compete, you probably won't be able to give your best. You also know that preparation involves more than just practicing hard the day or night before an event. It's about long-term dedication, focus, listening to coaches, conditioning, sharpening skills, analyzing your opponents, and practice, practice, practice. The same goes for preparing for exams.

> Preparation for tests should be ongoing. Waiting for the night before the test never works. You wind up being too tired to get anything done. Exams are, for the most part, no surprise. You know when they are coming, what material will be tested, and what you can do to prepare, so start early!
>
> — Becky Hunnewell

ANTICIPATION. You never know in advance exactly what's going to happen in an athletic competition. But if you have a good sense of what to expect from your opponents, you can focus on preparing for their general tendencies and on the specific challenges you're likely to face. It's the same with exams. Try to anticipate what will be on a test. If you were making up the exam, what kinds of questions would you ask? Would you be able to answer them? Based on what the professor stressed in class and in the reading assigned, what types of questions are likely to be included? What kinds of questions were asked on previous exams? If there will be essays, what kind of thinking and analysis might be expected? For example, you may have heard the term *critical thinking*. In college, it's likely that your professors will expect you to push your thinking harder and further and respond to questions more comprehensively and in more depth than your teachers did in high school. That means you might be asked questions in which you are expected to discuss, analyze, evaluate, or compare. If you're aware of this in advance, you can prepare in ways that will help you provide better responses.

If you don't practice, you'll never win a race, score a goal, or get a touchdown. Practice makes perfect. Make yourself an exam of what you think may be on the test. Then bring it to the professor or TA and ask if you're on the right track. Find all the right answers to that test and take it a few times.

— Jenifer Martin-Flake

Do as many practice exams as are available! Often professors post practice exams on the Internet, or some lucky students have previous years' exams from friends who have taken the course before. Often the professors keep very similar questions on exams because it's easier than making up a whole new exam.

— Erin McIntyre

TIME-OUT!

Select one class you are taking and pretend you are the professor. Make up an exam based on the work the class has done. Include at least 15 short-answer questions and two essay questions. Then answer them.

TAKE ADVANTAGE OF YOUR PROFESSORS' KINDNESS. Believe it or not, most professors want you to do well. If you do well, it means that they did a good job of teaching. So ask your professors what to expect—what material will be covered, how long the exam will be, and what types of questions may be asked (e.g., multiple choice, true/false, matching, fill-in, sentence completion, essay, etc.). As Erin McIntyre says, some professors post practice exams online. Others may make hard copies of previous exams available for you to study or hold review sessions before exams. When these review sessions are offered, be sure to attend. And never miss the last class session before a test. You never know what useful tidbits might be given out.

LEARN FROM OTHER STUDENTS. When studying for exams, other students can provide valuable assistance. Chapter 9 discusses the positives and negatives of study groups. In preparing for exams, it might be beneficial to study with one or more classmates, especially if your study mates are doing well in the course. But close to exam time when fellow students may be especially stressed, be careful not to let their anxieties rub off on you. Whether you decide to study alone or with others, it's a good idea to try out study methods and learning aids that have proven useful to academically strong students, like our contributors.

Going through previous exams with a group is extremely beneficial to compare answers and help each other if you get stuck. And going over examples done in class, homework problems, and examples in the book reinforces ways to approach a variety of problems.

— Erin McIntyre

I make flash cards that come from important vocabulary from the chapter. This type of association helps when it's time to take a test. It's also a good idea to grab a friend and quiz each other—it's a fun way to study!

— Jennifer Johnstone

In the week prior to an exam, I type up a study guide for myself containing the important material from my lecture notes. Typing the notes helps me study and makes them easier to go over later. I also make flash cards sometimes, mostly to rewrite the information. Once I've made flash cards and a study guide, I have a good feel for the material.

— Katie Younglove

To prepare for a test, I recommend taking the time to rewrite your notes in a condensed form. That way you must have a general understanding in order to shorten the material. Also, you begin to realize where you are missing information. You can then go back to your text, classmates, or other resources to fill the holes.

— Patricia Metzger

TIME-OUT!

Speak with three academically successful juniors or seniors. What study methods do they find work best? Which of these might work for you?

WHAT ABOUT CRAMMING AND OVERSTUDYING? You know that overtraining right before you compete can hamper your performance. But at the same time, not training enough can also lead to poor performance. Just as each athlete has to figure out what training regimen works best to maximize performance, each student has to figure out what study regimen enables him or her to achieve maximum performance on tests. There's no one right way. The key is doing what is necessary for you to feel comfortable with the material, knowing when you need to do more, and knowing when enough is enough.

> Try not to procrastinate. You really have to plan ahead. If you have a game on Friday and a night class Thursday, you have to study Monday, Tuesday, and Wednesday night to compensate. If you don't plan out chunks of time to study, you will be caught with no time and have to cram the night before. That's better than nothing, but it's not going to be very successful.
>
> — Darci Pemberton Desilet

> Always overprepare for the first exam of every course. When I have a new professor I don't know what to expect, so I make sure that I know everything that could possibly be on the test. I try to imagine that it will be the hardest, longest, and worst test I have ever taken. This allows me to get off to a good start by doing well on the first test and also helps me build momentum for the rest of the semester.
>
> — Julie Ruff

> When you feel confident with the material, walk away from it. Do not overstudy because you will question yourself too much during the exam.
>
> — Patricia Metzger

IT'S NOT ENOUGH TO BE AWAKE. YOU NEED TO BE ALERT. Remember to eat healthfully, stay hydrated, and get enough sleep during heavy study periods. The temptation is to do the exact opposite. You might be tempted to pull an all-nighter to cram for an exam with the help of cold showers, gallons of caffeinated beverages, bags of junk food, and even chemical stimulants, but it's not a good idea. These may keep you awake but certainly not alert. After a while, you end up just staring at your open books. And to make matters worse, for the next day or two you're too wiped out to do anything at all.

> The night before a test should be spent reviewing all of the related material, but get to bed at your normal time. There is nothing harder than trying to take a test when all you really want to do is go to sleep. Trying to cram the night before the test can not only have a negative influence on how you do on your test, but it will inevitably hinder your ability to perform at practice the next day.
>
> — Seth Neumuller

HOW IMPORTANT IS THE EXAM? In theory, every test and assignment is important. But in reality, some are more important than others. So be aware of how much weight each exam or assignment carries in the computation of your course grade. For example, if it's a midterm or final exam that counts for 30–40% or more of your grade, you probably want to put more effort into preparation than for a quiz or minor exam that only counts for 10–15%. But be careful. Don't ever just "blow it off" and fail to study for a test or quiz that "only" counts for a small percentage of your grade. Those 10–15%'s add up and can help compensate if you don't do as well as you'd like on a major exam. Doing well on minor tests and quizzes can easily make the difference between a good grade and a mediocre one, or even between passing or failing a course. Also, even if an exam carries little weight but is part of an important course—for example, a course in your major or one that's required for graduate school—put more time into studying.

THINK POSITIVELY. We've said it before, but it's worth repeating: If you go into a competition thinking your opposition is going to get the best of you, chances are you aren't going to perform as you are capable of. The same goes for taking an exam. If you've prepared properly, an exam is simply an opportunity for you to demonstrate how well you've learned the material. So go into an exam focused on what you know and how well you know it, expecting to win. Get pumped to a level that works for you—not overly so, where you're overwhelmed, but to a level that prepares you emotionally to do your best. You know what it feels like in athletics. Try to have that same feeling as you enter the exam room.

> If you invest sufficient time and effort in preparing for a situation, be it a class, an exam, or a race, you can approach the situation with confidence and succeed.
>
> — Mariko Tansey Holbrook

SOME TEST ANXIETY IS NORMAL. With exams, as with athletic competition, a certain amount of tension and arousal is natural. In fact, it's necessary to perform at your best. But extreme worry, anxiety, or fear can lead to poor performance. In athletics, you probably learned techniques to manage and reduce the negative impact of stress. These techniques can also be used to reduce test anxiety. If you need help in managing test-related stress and anxiety, speak with your Academic Advisor for Athletes, the staff at your school's counseling center, or your team's consulting sports psychologist about stress reduction/management and relaxation techniques.

> Some stress is OK because it gets you into gear. But I have found that during an exam, the information comes when I'm not stressing about the potential outcome. Frankly, there's nothing you can do when the test is in front of you except take it. Don't worry about the grade ahead of time. Concentrate on the questions themselves, and you might be surprised at how much you do know.
>
> — Angela Whyte

THERE IS NO EXCUSE FOR UNEXCUSED ABSENCES FROM EXAMS. In college, you usually know well in advance when exams and quizzes will be given. And it's your responsibility to be there. As soon as you're given dates and times of exams, mark them on your schedule, highlight them, and begin thinking about how and when you need to prepare to take them. If there are conflicts with your team's events or travel schedule, inform your professor immediately and discuss what alternatives can be worked out. These will depend on the professor's flexibility, which you can't automatically assume. So be respectful when requesting any special accommodations. It's also a good idea to consult with your team's Academic Advisor for Athletes about possible alternatives and to be sure you fully understand your school's policy on making up exams missed because of athletic conflicts. Your Academic Advisor for Athletes can also talk to the professor on your behalf if your discussions with him or her haven't resolved the situation.

IT IS USUALLY POSSIBLE TO RESOLVE SCHEDULING CONFLICTS. Here are some ways of handling it when you have to miss an exam because of a documented conflict: You may be permitted to take the exam earlier than other students, have the exam proctored or e-mailed to you while you're on the road, take the same or different exam when you return, complete an alternative assignment, or skip the exam altogether and have other exams and assignments carry more weight. But remember, never burden your professors with *your* problems, and never use your athletic issues (fatigue, team meeting, media interview, extra practice session) as an excuse for missing an exam or any other academic deadline. If you do, you will most likely receive an automatic F on the exam and seriously jeopardize your grade for the course as well as your relationship with that professor.

It's Game Time! Exam Day Preparation

BE READY PHYSICALLY. Treat exam days like game days. Make sure you get a good night's sleep, eat a nourishing breakfast and/or lunch, and be careful about taking any medication that will affect your ability to focus. You may even want to do some light exercise right before the exam, just to get the juices flowing. In addition, dress comfortably, and be sure to have with you whatever supplies you may need—pens, pencils, paper, erasers, calculators, eyeglasses, and study notes (but only if it's an open-book or open-notes exam). And don't forget that bottle of cold water (if it's allowed) and a watch or other way to keep track of time. It's also a good idea to make a just-in-case stop at the rest room *before* entering the exam, so you don't have to waste time during the exam or be uncomfortable because your professor won't allow you to leave the room once the exam has begun.

ARRIVE ON TIME OR EARLY. Getting to the exam room early enables you to select a seat where you'll feel most comfortable (e.g., near an open window if you'd like fresh air). Try to avoid listening to students who are frantic about the exam or nervously sharing all that they know with other students just before the exam begins. They'll only make you more stressed than you might already be. Take a few moments to breathe deeply and clear your mind of distracting thoughts. You want to be as relaxed and focused as possible.

> I like to arrive early to get an aisle seat where I don't feel so claustrophobic, and it's easier to ask questions from an outside seat. Also, I would recommend not sitting next to your teammates, especially if you're wearing athletic gear—there's less of a chance you will be accused of cheating.
>
> — Katie Younglove

> When it comes to exams, the key is to focus: Relax. If you don't know it by the time the test is in front of you, a light isn't going to shine down on you and give you the answers. Therefore, all you can do is your best. This is your time to prove to the professor that you really grasped the material in the course.
>
> — Audra Lissell

PRAYING MAY HELP. Just as you may feel that prayer is helpful and comforting in other aspects of your life, if you feel it will help you be more successful in taking an exam, go ahead and pray.

> Right before I take a test, I say a prayer and take a breath to gather myself, and then I make the best answer choices.
>
> — A. David Alston

WHAT IS YOUR PROFESSOR ASKING YOU TO DO? It's tempting to leap right in and begin answering questions as soon as the exam is in front of you. But unless you know exactly what the professor wants you to do, you could easily end up wasting time on questions you don't have to answer, leaving you with too little time to do a good job on those that are required. The first thing to do when you receive an exam is *carefully read and be sure you understand the instructions, and follow them.* If you have a choice of answering some questions and not others, for example, "Select three out of five essay questions," or "Answer 50 of the 55 multiple-choice questions," write three, not four or five essays (and choose the three you'll do the best job on), or answer the 50 multiple-choice questions you're most likely to get correct, not all 55, unless the instructions specify you can earn extra credit for your efforts. By the same token, if the professor or teaching assistant makes any announcements at the beginning of the exam, pay close attention or you may miss a useful hint or two. If there's anything you're not clear about, ask for clarification. Chances are you're not the only one who doesn't understand, and your classmates will appreciate your speaking up.

HOW MUCH TIME DO YOU HAVE? Once you fully understand the instructions, look over the whole test to determine the number of points each question or section of the exam is worth. Then make a plan for how much time you will devote to each section and/or question. The more points a question or section carries, the more time you'll want to devote to it. And stick to your plan. Check the time regularly to make sure you don't spend too long agonizing over relatively low-value questions, forcing you to rush through those that are worth more because time has nearly run out. Take a few deep breaths and exhale slowly. Now you're ready to begin writing.

> Try to watch the clock, making sure you won't be jammed for time at the end of the exam. But at the same time, don't rush through the exam and overlook the obvious. Exams are typically laid out such that they will be able to be completed on time.
>
> — Audra Lissell

DIFFERENT TYPES OF EXAM QUESTIONS. Most written tests are made up of *objective* or *short-answer* questions (e.g., multiple choice, true/false, matching, definitions, or fill-in-the-blank/sentence completion), *essay* questions, or a combination of the two. Essay exams may also be given in class where you are permitted to use notes and/or your book (often called an open-book or open-notes exam) or as take-home exams where you are given the question in class (or online) but write it outside of class and submit it to the professor by a specified date and time.

Objective questions usually ask you to recall specific pieces of information. As a rule, there is only one best answer that you must give to receive credit. If you know in advance that an exam will be made up primarily of objective questions, focus your studying on memorizing as many of the facts, definitions, and details presented in the text and in class as possible.

Essay questions, in contrast, give you more of a chance to demonstrate how you use the knowledge you've gained in class and from readings to address issues more comprehensively and in-depth. A higher level of critical thinking and creativity are generally expected. So when you're studying for an essay exam, focus more on the big ideas and larger picture. Try to analyze the information to get a strong handle on how the ideas and issues presented in the readings and in class fit together. You may also have a professor who gives exams where he or she asks you to respond orally to questions rather than write them out. Think of your responses as spoken essays, and prepare the same way as for a regular essay exam. Here are a few hints for each type of exam question.

Helpful Hints: Objective Questions

MULTIPLE CHOICE. Read each question carefully, and try to figure out the correct answer on your own. Then, after looking at the choices, select the answer that is closest to your initial response. If you aren't certain of the right answer or the one you first thought to be correct isn't listed, narrow the possibilities by eliminating the choices you know are definitely incorrect and select the one that makes the most sense to you. Remember, you don't have to work on questions in the order they appear on the exam. Don't waste too much time on questions you have trouble with. You can leave the difficult ones unanswered at first. Just be sure to make a mark next to the questions you skipped and return to them later. Some students prefer to answer the difficult questions as best they can and place a mark next to them. Then they can return to them if they have time. That way, if they run out of time, at least they've answered the questions rather than leaving them blank. Either way, the idea is not to linger so long on questions you have trouble with that you run out of time before getting to ones that are easy for you. And as you answer questions, look for hints or wording that may help you answer the ones you had difficulty with when you return to them. Be especially careful of key words such as *always, never, every,* and *some,* which, although they may make the question a bit more challenging, can also help you eliminate some of the choices.

TRUE/FALSE. Follow the same strategy with true/false questions as when you're dealing with multiple-choice questions. Don't dawdle on questions you're not sure about. Skip them or take a guess, but put a mark next to the ones you don't answer or aren't certain of, so you can return and work on them later, time permitting. And remember, for a statement to be *true, all* parts of the statement have to be true. If any part of the statement is false, then the statement is *false.*

MATCHING. The key to matching-type questions is to understand the concepts or terms you're being asked to match, and then figure out what they have in common. Begin with one of the lists or columns as your starting point; then match items from the other list or column to it. Narrow down your choices by first making the matches you're certain are correct. Cross off items as you use them. Then work with the items you have left, making educated guesses if you have to. Again, it's a good idea to make a mark next to the answers or items you're not sure about or leave out, and then return to them later. Also, as you go through the rest of the exam, look for information or tips from other questions that will help you make the correct matches.

FILL-IN AND SENTENCE COMPLETION. These types of questions can be especially challenging because you aren't given a list of possibilities from which to choose your response. You have to know the answer or at least one that's close. If you don't know the answer, write down one you think makes the most sense. With luck, your answer might be close enough to receive partial credit.

Helpful Hints: Essay-Type Questions

WHAT IS AN ESSAY? Many students are intimidated by the very word *essay,* and the prospect of having to write one makes them very nervous. That's because they don't understand what an essay really is. In truth, *essay* is just a fancy, highbrow word for *story.* So when your professors ask you to write an essay, all they're doing is asking you to tell a (usually nonfiction) story on paper that deals with the issues and ideas in the questions they pose. Think of the question as giving you the basic plot of the story. With that in mind, your job is to develop a story line and provide enough connected details so that someone who reads the essay will understand, appreciate, and be informed about the story's underlying plot. In other words, as with any story, you want to make sure that your essay communicates and connects with the reader.

WHERE TO BEGIN. Every story has to begin somewhere, and essays begin with the questions your professors ask. So read them carefully and be sure you understand what you are being asked to do. If the exam requires you to write a number of essays, read and think about each of the questions and decide which is the easiest for you to handle, next easiest, and so on. Then respond to them in that order.

Before you start writing, ask yourself, *What do I want to say? Why should the reader care?* It's not a good idea to begin writing an essay before you have a solid handle on what you want to say. So after reading the question, organize your thoughts on a piece of scrap paper by jotting down a list of points you want to make or main ideas you want to cover (it doesn't have to be in outline form, but it can be). As you're doing this, ask yourself questions like "Is this idea important?" "What makes it so?" "Will the reader understand?" "Why should he or she care about it?" Then go back to the question and make sure that what you plan to say responds directly to it. Time is limited, so be careful that your essay focuses on the topic and doesn't contain a lot of extraneous material. Keep in mind that essay questions most often ask you to provide information and/or analysis, not opinion. So unless the question specifically asks for your opinion, don't give it. To be on the safe side, avoid statements that begin with "I think," "I believe," "I feel," or "In my opinion." In fact, stay away from the word "I" altogether.

USE THE QUESTION IN PREPARING YOUR ANSWER. Essay questions usually ask you to *describe, compare and contrast, discuss, evaluate, analyze,* or *take and support a position.* Your job is to "Just do it!" Give the professor exactly what the key words ask for. Don't be afraid to use the question in your answer. For example, many fine essays begin with a topic sentence that basically restates the key issues raised in the question (e.g., This paper will compare and contrast _____ with _____). This is a straightforward way to connect the reader with the question and introduce your main ideas. Then, using the question to guide you, tell a story in the essay that demonstrates you have been thinking about what you've been taught. Develop your ideas in as logical and comprehensive a response as you can, citing readings, class discussions, lecture material, and when appropriate, your own ideas.

READABILITY. Even though you only have to write one exam, your professor may have to read hundreds. The easier you make it for your professors to read your essays, the friendlier reading you're likely to get. However, if your exam is a chore to read, it may also be a chore for your professor to give it a high grade. Label each response by letter or number in your exam book, and write as legibly as possible. And remember, an essay is not an instant message or text message. Spell out words fully and properly (i.e., you, not "u"), and write complete, grammatically correct sentences because grammar and spelling *do* count. Grammatical or spelling errors can lower your grade dramatically. Before you hand in your exam, if time permits, proofread what you've written and make corrections where needed.

OPEN-BOOK, OPEN-NOTES, AND TAKE-HOME EXAMS. When they hear that an exam will be open-book, open-note, or take-home, many students think it means they don't have to study. But they are wrong! Being allowed to refer to the text or your notes during an exam isn't much help if you're not familiar with the material that's in them or if you don't have a solid understanding of what it all means and how it relates. What's more, because students have the opportunity to use books, notes, and other materials without having to rely on memorization, professors generally expect students to write essays that are significantly more comprehensive in breadth and depth. On the one hand, open-book and open-notes exams mean you don't have to memorize all kinds of information, and in the case of take-homes, the questions aren't a surprise. But on the other hand, you're expected to submit work that is of significantly higher quality. Also, be careful when you are writing open-book, open-notes, and take-home assignments. Don't ever take words directly from a book or other source and use them as if they were your own. If you do, it's plagiarism, an extremely serious academic offense that could lead to expulsion from school. Whenever you use phrases, sentences, or paragraphs that aren't actually your own words, make certain you include a citation that tells the reader where they are from and gives credit to the original author.

ORAL EXAMS. Although oral exams aren't common, there's a chance you'll have to take one at some point in your college career. If you do, prepare for it the way you would a written essay exam. Study to get a grasp of the big ideas and how they relate. Then, after the professor asks the question, take a moment to process the question and organize your thoughts before you respond. If you don't understand the question, ask the professor to clarify or rephrase it. It can feel like a very pressurized situation, but try to stay calm and focused. And when you answer, speak clearly and with as much confidence as you can muster.

TIME-OUT!

Which type of exam do you prefer? Which do you like least? What can you do to become more positive about the latter?

Handling Other Issues

RUNNING OUT OF TIME? Don't panic. Unless there are penalties for wrong answers, answer every objective question, even if it means guessing at the last minute. You'll at least stand a chance of earning more points than if you'd left the answers blank. With essay questions, if you don't have enough time to complete your response, make a few key points in outline form to demonstrate you know the critical ideas your professor is looking for. By doing this, you may earn partial credit—again, certainly more than if you don't address the ideas at all. You may also want to let your professor know you ran out of time and, if possible, would appreciate the opportunity to address the remaining question(s) at a later date. After all, there's no harm in asking.

FINISHED EARLY. Don't be in a rush to leave. Once you've completed the exam, make sure you followed instructions carefully and answered all the questions. Go back to the difficult questions you marked earlier, review your answers, proofread and correct your writing, and add additional information to make your answers more comprehensive. If, for example, an essay has subparts, check to be certain you've responded to each of them. But be careful about changing your answers, especially to multiple-choice questions. Your initial response is most often the best answer.

BRAIN LOCK. In the event that your mind becomes blocked in the middle of an exam, try this technique: Put your pen down, close your eyes, take a deep breath, and let it out slowly. Listen to and feel yourself breathing. Repeat the deep breaths three or four more times, then return to the test. If you frequently feel a sense of panic during or right before an exam, seek help with stress reduction/management on campus (see chapter 3).

A WORD ABOUT CHEATING: *DON'T.* There may be times when you feel like your back is up against the wall. It's the peak of your season, you haven't had any time to study, your grades have been hurting, and your eligibility is on the line. You might be tempted to cheat on an exam. But no matter how tempting or how low the odds of getting caught, *Don't do it!* Academic integrity and honesty are core values on college campuses. Whether or not you get caught, cheating is wrong. It will communicate a negative impression to your classmates and friends, reflect badly on other student-athletes by reinforcing the dumb jock stereotype, lower your self-esteem, and devalue your education. And if you get caught, the penalties could be devastating. You risk getting bounced out of your major, thrown off the team and losing your scholarship, or kicked out of school. So when it comes to cheating, the word is *Don't!*

TIME-OUT!

What is your school's policy on cheating and plagiarism? Is there an academic honor code and a judicial system to protect students and govern their behavior?

Postexam Review

EVALUATING YOUR PERFORMANCE. After practice or competition, it's standard to review and evaluate what took place to improve future performance. What worked and what needs improvement? Where did the team or individual competitors come up short? Why? What adjustments are needed for the next event? After an exam, the same kind of review and evaluation is very useful as well, and for the same reason—to improve future performance. Whether you did well or not, much can be learned by reviewing a recently graded exam. So even though you might be tempted to bury the exam deep in a desk drawer or crumple it up and toss it in the trash, don't. Look it over carefully and learn from it. Ask yourself some questions: first about your preparation, then about how you handled the exam itself. For example, did I study the right material? Was I prepared adequately, and if not, how might I have prepared better? Were my class notes weak, or did I miss reading the essential information? Where did I lose points, and why? Was it because I didn't understand the question, didn't know the material, or expressed myself poorly? Did I follow the instructions? Were there certain types of questions I found particularly difficult? Which types of questions did I do well on, and why? And then, of course, the bottom-line question: What do I need to do differently next time?

GO RIGHT TO THE SOURCE. If you did poorly on an exam, you may be reluctant, embarrassed, or even fearful about meeting with your professor or TA. But they are the people who are in the best position to help you evaluate and improve your performance. As soon as possible after receiving your exam back, while the material is still fresh in your mind, make an appointment to review your exam. Ask for an explanation of where you fell short and where you did a better job, but be careful not to come on too strongly or use too hostile a tone. Aggressively seeking a review rarely does anyone any good, especially if your efforts are perceived as merely trying to get your grade raised. But a manner that communicates a genuine interest in benefiting from feedback will more likely result in your professor carefully revisiting your exam responses. The review will be more helpful to you, and he or she may even provide suggestions on how to improve your performance on the next exam. Take careful notes throughout the review, and use them when preparing for the next test. On top of everything else, this will also demonstrate to your professor or TA that you truly care about mastering the course material.

Accommodations for Students with a Disability

IF YOU HAVE A DISABILITY, DON'T HIDE IT. If earlier in your school career you were diagnosed as having a disability that handicaps you when taking exams under regular conditions, you may be entitled to special accommodations for testing. Unfortunately, many students don't take advantage of this opportunity because they don't want to identify themselves as different. This is especially true of athletes who think they must project an image of strength, self-reliance, or even perfection. What happens is that during an exam, the disability interferes with their ability to demonstrate how much of the material they have actually learned, and their grades suffer, not because they don't know the material but because their disability keeps them from showing it.

ADVOCATE FOR YOURSELF. In compliance with mandates of the U.S. Office for Civil Rights and U.S. Department of Education (Section 504 of the 1973 Federal

Rehabilitation Act) and the 1990 Americans with Disabilities Act, colleges are required to guarantee that students aren't disadvantaged in taking exams by virtue of having a disability. For example, if you have been diagnosed with a visual problem or learning disability and read or write slowly, you may be entitled to have reading material recorded on tapes, receive extended time, or have no time limit on exams. If you have difficulty hearing because of a previously diagnosed hearing impairment and can't hear classroom lectures and discussions, you may be entitled to have someone take notes for you in class. Accommodations such as these are generally reviewed and approved by your school's Office of Disability Services in consultation with you, your Academic Advisor for Athletes, and your professor. The key is to understand what your special needs are, to make those needs known very early in the semester, and to advocate for yourself to ensure that they are met. Just as you always want to compete on an equal playing field with other athletes, you have the right to expect the same kind of equality in the classroom without being disadvantaged because of your special needs. Don't be afraid to speak up for yourself.

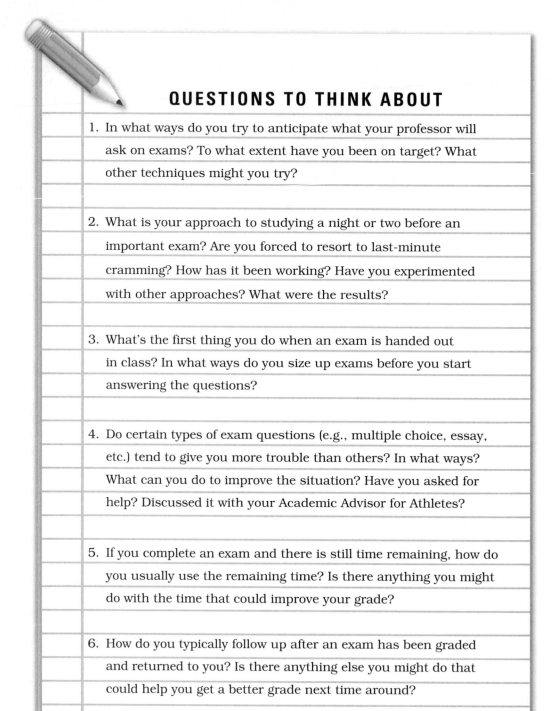

QUESTIONS TO THINK ABOUT

1. In what ways do you try to anticipate what your professor will ask on exams? To what extent have you been on target? What other techniques might you try?

2. What is your approach to studying a night or two before an important exam? Are you forced to resort to last-minute cramming? How has it been working? Have you experimented with other approaches? What were the results?

3. What's the first thing you do when an exam is handed out in class? In what ways do you size up exams before you start answering the questions?

4. Do certain types of exam questions (e.g., multiple choice, essay, etc.) tend to give you more trouble than others? In what ways? What can you do to improve the situation? Have you asked for help? Discussed it with your Academic Advisor for Athletes?

5. If you complete an exam and there is still time remaining, how do you usually use the remaining time? Is there anything you might do with the time that could improve your grade?

6. How do you typically follow up after an exam has been graded and returned to you? Is there anything else you might do that could help you get a better grade next time around?

CHAPTER 11

Mind–Body Connection

Taking Good Care of Yourself*

As an athlete, your first priority should be your health. It is important to eat all necessary meals and provide yourself with ample sleep. Alcohol and drugs will only make it harder to perform and should not be included in a healthy lifestyle.

— Jennifer Johnstone

If you believe the hype, you might think that all it takes to raise your GPA, become a better athlete, eliminate stress, energize yourself, and live a more fulfilling life is taking the right supplements. It sounds so simple. But don't waste your money or risk your health. These goals can't be bought, and you certainly won't get them from magical pills, powders, or serums. However, *benefits like these are attainable and under your control!* By developing the habits of taking good care of yourself and working toward optimum wellness, you can benefit both academically and athletically.

Taking good care of yourself is about self-awareness and attitude—intellectual, emotional, social, and spiritual. And it's about making consistently wise health-related decisions, based on the most reliable, current information.

The critical areas that relate to taking good care of yourself as a student-athlete are sleep, nutrition, physical health, stress management, use and abuse of legal and illegal drugs, addictions, and sexuality. During college, you'll get a great deal of advice from family, coaches, trainers, professors, teammates, friends, and others. And you may do your own reading and research. Everyone sounds like he or she knows the pathway to maximum health and wellness. The problem is, everyone tells you something different.

The authors wish to acknowledge Dr. Barry Poris, associate professor of health and physical education, Long Island University–Brooklyn Campus, for his expertise and invaluable contributions in the preparation of this chapter.

To be successful, your approach to optimum wellness must be well thought out, carefully planned and implemented, and evaluated over time. The keys to success are balance, moderation, and variation. An example of *balance* might be maintaining the right amount of exercise and fitness training so that you are physically ready to carry out your team responsibilities, but at the same time making sure that you get enough rest. *Moderation* means avoiding extremes; for example, run 3 miles a day on a wooden gym floor for cardiovascular fitness instead of 10 miles a day on a paved surface that might be harmful to your knees or ankles. Too much of a good thing *can* be bad! Examples of *variation* might be not eating the same foods at every meal or diversifying your routine so you don't do the same exercises each and every day. Why not mix it up? It will be more stimulating to your muscles and your palate.

There is no magic to achieving optimum wellness. Because everyone is different, you have to figure out what works for you—for your mind and body—and stick to it as closely as possible. It's a lifelong process that involves wise decision making and good habits. The payoffs will come academically and athletically while you're in college, as well as with better health and performance for the rest of your life.

> Pay attention and learn how your body works. . . . There will be an adjustment period to get used to training, but find what works for you and what gives you results. Get enough sleep, eat healthy, and maintain a balance with mind and body.
>
> — Lauren Fendrick

Tips from Peers and Profs

Get Enough Sleep

WHY WASTE TIME SLEEPING? To function at your best, you probably need to spend about a third of your life sleeping. On top of causing you to feel tired and out of it much of the time, lack of sleep can affect concentration, memory, decision making, mood, and tolerance for others. People who lack sleep often feel overwhelmed by even the smallest tasks and have a short fuse. They also tend to have slower reflexes and are prone to making more mistakes. Being sleep deprived causes serious difficulties in the classroom, in your sport, and in your relationships with others. In addition, insufficient sleep is linked with developing clinical depression.

TOO MUCH SLEEP CAN ALSO BE A PROBLEM. If day after day, for no clear-cut physical reason, you just can't bring yourself to get out of bed, it could be a sign of serious underlying psychological issues. So if you see yourself or others lapsing into this pattern, be sure it's dealt with as soon as possible (see chapter 3 for resources).

FIGURE OUT HOW MUCH SLEEP YOU NEED. The need for sleep varies from individual to individual, ranging from 6 to 10 hours a night with the average about $7\frac{1}{2}$. Some students find that a short power nap of 20 to 30 minutes during the day helps reenergize them, but others don't.

> The number-one thing is to learn how to schedule in enough sleep in your day. You need your rest to perform at your full potential, whether in your academics or athletics.
>
> — Nate Jones
>
> My body is programmed to shut down about 10:30 at night. I beg other athletes: Listen to your bodies. Do not force yourself to stay awake.
>
> — Courtney Turner

TIME-OUT!

For the next week, keep a chart of your sleep patterns: when you go to bed at night, how long it takes to fall asleep, whether you sleep through the night, what time you wake up in the morning, and naps. Note if there's a difference in how you feel and perform based on sleep patterns. What does this tell you? Are changes needed?

BE CONSISTENT. Once you figure out how much sleep works best for you, try to keep regular hours for bedtime and waking, staying as close as possible to this schedule on weekdays as well as on weekends.

> Sleep is key. Seven hours is great, and also going to bed at the same time every night is good for your biological clock. That way you get tired at the same time every night and will have a great night's sleep.
>
> — Abraham Billy Hardee III

DEVELOP A SLEEP RITUAL. Your body and mind become better adjusted to the transition from wakefulness to sleep if you have a sleep ritual. When your team is traveling, however, a sleep ritual may be difficult to maintain. Meditating, reading, drinking a cup of herbal tea, listening to soothing music, taking a bath, or even exercising lightly before lying down works for some students. Avoid sleeping pills and other depressant substances. They can be habit forming, dangerous, and leave you with a hangover in the morning.

> On the road it's rougher to stick to your routine because of time changes and flights. I would let myself sleep as much as possible on the planes or buses because people never sleep as well on the road as they do in their own bed.
>
> — Ashley Ready

SUBSTANCES THAT AFFECT SLEEP. Foods that are difficult to digest, like fatty and spicy ones, as well as those with high sugar content, caffeinated foods and beverages (be aware of hidden caffeine in chocolate and soda), alcohol, and tobacco can interfere with sleep quality. Also, medications such as weight loss pills, some decongestants, and cold/flu medicines containing caffeine can have stimulating effects that inhibit sleep. Be aware, too, of the possible cumulative effect of these substances. Although you may not realize it, a buildup over the course of the day can have an impact on your ability to sleep well at night.

TIME-OUT!

Pinpoint a night within the last few weeks when you had trouble falling asleep. What do you think was the cause? What did you do? What could you have done that might have avoided the problem? If it's a continuing problem, what steps will you take to deal with it?

Eat Well and Wisely

SEEK EXPERT ADVICE. Put aside all the fad diets currently on the market. Research indicates that sound nutrition is derived from a diet containing 55% to 60% whole grains, 30% fat (with only 10% saturated and the intake of trans fats kept as low as possible), and 10% to 15% protein. In addition, the U.S. Department of Agriculture's "MyPyramid" (www.mypyramid.gov), which in 2005 replaced the long-standing Food Guide Pyramid, provides numerous options to help you make healthy food choices. For example, protein should be derived from fish, poultry, beans, and nuts, with limited emphasis on red meats. Also remember, there are sources of calcium besides milk and cheese. Products such as green leafy vegetables and legumes are delicious alternatives to dairy.

WHAT'S GOOD FOR OTHERS MIGHT NOT BE THE BEST FOR YOU. Keep in mind that the USDA guidelines were written for the general public. As an athlete, your nutritional needs may be different. So you also need to seek out the best nutritional advice on campus. For example, an exercise physiologist or sports nutritionist may be able to design a diet that responds directly to your individual needs—the physical and nutritional demands of your sport, your body mass and body type, metabolic rate, gender, and age. Getting the best professional advice is especially important if you are concerned about bulking up or making weight, where you run the risk of seriously harming your body if you make poor decisions.

> A school nutritionist can help you manage your eating if you feel you need help. But the incentive to become the best student-athlete you can be should be the driving force behind making smart, healthy eating choices.
>
> — Audra Lissell
>
> Many athletes try to diet during the season, which is ridiculous because during the season is when you need most nutrients. Eating healthier, yes; cutting back on food, No!
>
> — Johanna DiChiara-Drab

TIME-OUT!

Go to the MyPyramid Web site. Print out the diet recommended for you. Click on "MyPyramid Tracker" for a detailed dietary and physical assessment. Print it out. How does your current diet stack up? Consult with a sports nutritionist on campus about what changes might be worth considering.

MAKE THE RIGHT CHOICES. It's generally a good idea to eat lots of fruits and vegetables, and don't forget, color is key. Choose brown rice and bread over white, sweet potatoes over white ones, and dark green leafy vegetables over lighter colored ones. Staples of your diet should include grains, pastas (be careful of rich and spicy sauces and gravies), rice, and potatoes (baked or boiled, not fried), as well as lean meat, poultry, fish, nuts, and low-fat milk, yogurt, and cheeses. Go for hot foods that are steamed, broiled, or baked, and limit your intake of fried foods. Choose fresh fruit, trail mix, or granola over candy bars or sugar-filled cereals. Drink water, fruit juice, or low-fat milk instead of soft drinks, caffeinated high-energy beverages, and coffee. Eat whole-wheat pretzels rather than fried potato chips. Avoid artery-clogging burgers, french fries, cakes, cookies, and ice cream. Read labels on processed foods and stay away from those made with hydrogenated and partially hydrogenated oils (trans fats), which have been linked to the development of cardiovascular disease. And be especially careful of overconsuming power bars and sports drinks. They don't take the place of a nutritious, well-balanced meal, and overhydrating can be dangerous.

> As long as you don't succumb to the all-you-can-eat desserts every night, you don't need to worry about the "freshman 15"* as much.
>
> — Mariko Tansey Holbrook

TIME-OUT!

Keep a list of *everything* you eat and drink for an entire day. Evaluate the wisdom of your choices.

QUANTITY COUNTS. Portion sizes are important factors in maintaining balanced nutrition and developing good eating habits. Too much of anything, even healthy choices, will not digest well or will get stored in your body as fat. Also, remember that the good eating habits you develop today are likely to stay with you for the rest of your life. That's important because although you might think you have a bottomless pit of a stomach and can eat anything and everything, as you get older your metabolism is likely to change. If you get into the habit of eating too much now, you could end up gaining a lot of extra weight later in life. So avoid the super-sized portions before they super-size *you*!

EAT SENSIBLY BEFORE THE BIG COMPETITION OR THE EXAM. Stick with what is easily digestible and contains the necessary nutrients. That burst of energy you might get from a candy bar or cup of coffee right before practice, competition, or an exam only lasts for a very short time before you crash and end up with less energy than you had before consuming it. Concentrating on whole grains and minimizing your intake of saturated fats and protein will make it easier on your digestive system while providing the long-lasting energy that you'll need. Drinking plenty of water provides necessary hydration and keeps your muscles working properly.

EATING ON THE ROAD. When you're away from campus, sticking with the diet that's right for you can be a real challenge. It's just too easy to get off track when you are eating on the road. So be especially careful and diligent.

---

*Campus wisdom has it that college students, particularly women, are likely to gain a quick 15 pounds their freshman year. That's because of changes in eating habits brought on by a variety of new stressors, eating on the run, overuse of soda and snack vending machines all over campus, as well as late-night beer, pizza, and other fast food binges. And, of course, Mom's no longer around to make sure her kids eat their veggies.

Remember, eating is part of your preparation for competition. You want to be fit, energized, and feeling your best, and much of it has to do with what and how much you eat and drink, no matter where you are.

> In airports, McDonald's and Burger King may be the only places you see to grab food. But a closer look reveals that many healthy snacks, like trail mixes, juices, and so on, can be purchased from little convenience stores. If you're going to enjoy a pizza, make it a reward *after* winning a game rather than an hour before one!
>
> — Audra Lissell

BE MINDFUL OF DISORDERED EATING—IN YOURSELF AND OTHERS. Doing anything to the extreme is risky, particularly when it comes to eating. Chronic dieting coupled with excessive exercising, periodic fasting, or binge eating followed by forced vomiting or the use of laxatives are indications of serious problems like anorexia nervosa or bulimia. These are psychological eating disorders, affecting mostly young women (although recently on the rise among young men), that can result in significant damage to the body and even death, if untreated.

ASK FOR HELP. How can you tell if you or a fellow student or teammate has an eating disorder or is at risk of developing one? Look for signs and symptoms such as constant loss of appetite, dysfunctional and/or compulsive eating patterns, low self-esteem, negative attitude, constant reference to poor body image, and/or a significant loss of weight to the point of emaciation. If you have even a faint suspicion that you or someone you know is exhibiting any of these signs, you have a responsibility to contact a coach, trainer, or other school official immediately. This situation requires prompt intervention by a trained professional.

Stay on Top of Your Physical and Emotional Health

YOU'RE NOT IMMUNE TO INJURY. More than half of all college athletes sustain an injury that results in being out of competition for an extended period of time. Then depending on the severity of the injury, the condition may spiral into additional symptoms and difficulties such as muscle tension, headaches, drowsiness from medication, gastrointestinal problems, difficulty sleeping, difficulty concentrating, and problems getting around campus. And when injury strikes, emotional issues may surface as well. Feelings related to no longer being part of the team, being out of the limelight, and losing the social status of being a college athlete are common. And there's the emotional stress that often results from so many unanswered questions: How long will the injury last? How much rehab will I need? How quickly can I get back to practice and competition? Will I ever get back to the level I was at before? And what about my athletic scholarship? If I lose that, will I be able to stay in school? These are very serious questions, issues, and considerations that have an impact on academics. After all, it's not easy to sit in class for extended periods of time or concentrate in the library when you're exhausted and hurting much of the time or worried about the kinds of questions just listed.

AN OUNCE OF PREVENTION. Do all that you can to avoid injury. Consult the latest reliable research, talk to the experts on campus, and work with your team's coaches and trainers to get yourself in the best possible shape for competition. Stick to your training regimen, and always follow proper techniques for lifting and exercising. Find the right balance: Avoid overdoing or underdoing it.

LISTEN TO YOUR BODY. You know your body much better than anyone else does. Understand the signals that tell you if the training you're doing is effective. Pay attention to how you feel during and after workouts. Learn the difference between muscle soreness and the pain of injury.

> The word *injury* is probably the most feared word in a college athlete's vocabulary. But it's something that nearly every athlete must deal with at some point. Whether it's a small muscle pull or a season-ending tear, the key is to stay positive. I know. I missed my entire freshman year with a back injury after having tried to "play through it." You have to know your limits. Don't try and tough it out when you're really hurt, but also don't try and use an injury as an excuse to get out of the "harder drills" during practice.
>
> — Audra Lissell

TAKE CHARGE. Take responsibility for your own health and fitness. It's not a good idea simply to turn your body over to a trainer, physical therapist, or doctor. There is not just one right training method to achieve fitness. So read up on the latest scientific information relevant to your own conditioning. Speak with experts on campus (e.g., sports science and exercise physiology faculty), and share your findings with trainers and coaches.

TIME-OUT!

Schedule a meeting with the person who oversees your conditioning to discuss the rationale underlying your regimen. Does it make sense to you? If not, discuss your concerns.

DON'T PLAY HURT. No athlete wants to appear weak or let the team down by being sidelined with an injury. And whether rightly or wrongly perceived, some college athletes feel pressure from coaches and/or teammates to train hard and compete even when hurt. Some fear getting cut from the team and losing their financial aid if they don't compete. So it's understandable that so many student-athletes go to great lengths to hide their injuries, tough it out, and play when they're injured. But in the long run, that can be dangerous. So trust your instincts and seek prompt attention from your team's sports medicine staff. Although it may be difficult, stand up to any pressures and resist the temptation to play if you're not physically ready.

> I had a situation where people did not listen to my injuries because, being black, my bruises didn't show, and I didn't swell much. But I knew I was *really* hurt. If athletes feel they are being forced to compete or train unsafely with an injury, they must see their sports doctor or trainer for assistance. This really saved me.
>
> — Courtney Turner

HEALING TAKES TIME. Be patient. Coming back too soon could result in further serious damage causing you to be out of action even longer or end your varsity career entirely. If you have to be out, try finding another way to contribute to your team.

> My junior year I was captain and was injured in the beginning of the season. I quickly had to change my role from being a leader by action to being a leader from the bench. Being injured is the hardest role to play. You feel so helpless. I dealt with my injuries by finding other ways to contribute. I became a student of the game to the highest extent. My coaches taught me how to scout players and different strategies of coaching.
>
> — Ashley Ready

GUT CHECK. It's quite normal to feel emotionally stressed at times, even for an extended period. If it happens, remember the personal characteristics we discussed in chapter 2. Commitment, focus, dedication, discipline, self-confidence, and courage have helped you get through rough times and kept you going in the past. So when life seems overwhelming, do a gut check. Remember that you're the same person you always have been, with the same positive attributes. Reach back and use them.

WHAT DID THE WATER COOLER, LOCKERS, OR WALLS EVER DO TO YOU? In chapter 2 you also learned some suggestions for managing stress, and we encouraged you to seek help from people on and off campus. Student-athletes, though, tend to avoid talking about their problems. They typically try to suck it up rather than risk being seen as weak, unstable, unable to handle pressure, or a head case. So instead of opening up and sharing their emotional issues, you've probably seen teammates throw things wildly, explode verbally, kick over the water cooler, punch lockers and walls, and throw tantrums. Blowing off steam may be helpful, but these are not the ways to do it. It's much better (and far more productive) to make use of the resources available on or off campus to manage stress (see chapter 3).

> It's okay to see a therapist and to recognize that you have been pushed beyond your limits, no matter what the contributing factors may be. As an athlete, your first priority is *you* and then everything else. In order to be well, you must take care of your mental health. This is key. If your mental health is strained, your physical health will be too.
>
> — Courtney Turner

TIME-OUT!

Describe three methods you use to manage athletic and/or academic stress. Are they socially appropriate? If not, what alternatives would be preferable?

Winning Isn't Worth Risking Your Health

GAINING AN EDGE BUT LOSING EVEN MORE. Athletes want to become stronger and faster, more muscular or leaner, and almost all look for ways to gain an edge over their competition. You probably do, too. We all want to win. And if yours is like most colleges, students may be able to obtain a variety of drugs—legal and illegal, prescription as well as over the counter—they think will do the trick. But do you want to enhance your performance in a healthful manner, or are you willing to risk serious medical problems to gain that edge? Anabolic steroids (e.g., THG, which made news because of the Balco investigation), steroid precursors (e.g., andro, admittedly used by former baseball slugger Mark McGuire), growth hormones, creatine, ephedrine, and a variety of over-the-counter nutritional and herbal supplements can be harmful. Tranquilizers, amphetamines, medications increasingly prescribed for students with attention-deficit disorder, and a host of other drugs, although helpful to some, may be dangerous for you. It's up to you to weigh the risks before giving in to the temptation.

SOME SUBSTANCES COULD END YOUR CAREER. As a college athlete, it's your responsibility to avoid substances banned by the NCAA. Whether prescribed by a physician or sold over the counter, don't assume that a medication is acceptable. For example, commonly used decongestants, headache remedies, and diet aids typically contain stimulants, which may be prohibited in your sport and could cause sleep problems. In addition, be sure to know the exact name of any medication you are considering taking because many products have similar names. For instance, Tylenol and Afrin nasal spray are permitted by the NCAA. But CoTylenol, Afrin tablets, and Afrinol contain prohibited substances. Before you take any medication, check with your coach or a member of your team's sports medicine staff to see if it is permitted. Ignorance is never an excuse. And remember that even if a substance isn't banned, it can still pose a health risk.

> The use of any drug, whether it is legal, illegal, prescription, over the counter, alcohol, or tobacco, is a personal choice, and you must be willing to deal with the consequences that may come from making that choice. No matter what the situation, identify the consequences, both positive and negative, and make an educated decision based on what could result from taking the drug. How will this help me? How may it harm me? Does taking this drug have any legal or moral implications? Those are all questions you must be able to answer before you use anything.
>
> — Jim Olds

ALTHOUGH THE LABEL SAYS "SAFE AND EFFECTIVE," IT MAY NOT BE. You've got to be very careful. Not everyone is affected the same way by the same drug. Factors such as your weight, how recently you ate before taking the medication, dosage (frequency and amount), and interaction with other drugs you may be taking have an impact on the effects a drug has on you. You can even be affected differently by the same drug at different times. Remember that every medication has side effects. Self-medicating can be dangerous. So consult your team physician before taking any medication.

PAIN KILLERS CAN KILL MORE THAN PAIN. As too many professional athletes have found, pain killers and anti-inflammatory drugs (even those sold over the counter) can be harmful. From naproxen and ibuprofen, to Vicodin, Celebrex, and OxyContin, use of these types of medication might help you feel better initially. But continued use could result in breathing difficulty, dizziness, disorientation, hearing loss, vomiting, heart disease, and kidney and liver failure. Developing a drug dependency is also possible, and overuse could kill you. *Be careful!*

Alcohol and Other Feel-Goods

NICOTINE: RESPONSIBLE FOR MORE DEATHS THAN ANY OTHER DRUG. The nicotine in tobacco is considered to be as addictive as crack cocaine. So giving up tobacco is far easier said than done. Smoking makes breathing more difficult and cuts down on endurance. And if you think chewing tobacco is a safer alternative, think again. Chewing tobacco has the same addictive qualities as cigarettes, and it causes cancer. The only difference is that you won't be harming anyone else with your secondhand smoke. Besides, it's likely that rules prohibit the use of any form of tobacco by athletes at your school. When it comes to marijuana, indications are that it may impair thinking, memory, and perception. Its use is prohibited by the NCAA and it's illegal. So it really isn't the benign substance many think it to be. Use it and you risk being thrown off the team, out of school, and into jail. Enough said.

"DRINKING RESPONSIBLY." You've heard it before: It's wise to avoid drinking alcoholic beverages altogether, and if you're underage, it's against the law to consume them. The fact is, alcohol is a toxic substance and potentially addictive. But if you are going to drink in spite of this, here are a few strategies to reduce the negative outcomes: Water down the drinks; don't drink on an empty stomach; sip, don't gulp; know your limit and stop before you even get close; don't provide drinks for others or encourage others to drink, especially if they're underage; and, of course, don't drink and drive. Better yet, why not become the designated driver whenever you're out?

> Personally, I don't take drugs or drink alcohol. I don't have the desire or the money.
>
> — Spencer Harris
>
> I eat three meals a day and I never drink. You have to be an idiot to jeopardize your college career for a $3 beverage.
>
> — Abraham Billy Hardee III

SO-CALLED HEALTHY DRUGS. The herbal supplements you hear so much about—many with healthy-sounding names that are sold in vitamin stores, health food shops, and regular pharmacies–can be harmful, even *deadly. Natural* and *herbal* do not necessarily mean good for you. Ephedrine, St. John's wort, ginseng, and the various power bars, protein bars, energy drinks, and sleep enhancers are not regulated by the federal government. Claims of increased strength, improved performance, and enhanced well-being may have no scientific or medical validity. Supplements aren't necessarily tested on human subjects, and because they aren't considered food, they aren't required to meet regulations pertaining to product claims or food labeling.

According to the U.S. Anti-Doping Agency (USADA), it's impossible to be absolutely sure about a supplement's contents (usually listed in fine print on the label in milligrams) so be very suspicious of any supplement claims that include the terms *ripped, energy, nondrowsy, fuel, metabolic enhancer, weight loss, growth,* and *increased strength.* And we'll add *megadose* to the list.

WHAT'S NOT ON THE LABEL? None of the supplement labels tell you that they may have serious long-term effects. In men, they can stifle bone growth and lead to testicular shrinkage, liver tumors, development of breasts, infertility, and accelerated growth of prostate cancer. In women, they can cause male pattern baldness, excessive facial hair, deepened voice, and abnormal menstruation. These may not appear for 20 to 30 years. Others, like ephedra, suppress appetite and ensure weight loss, but they have been linked to psychotic episodes, hypertension, heatstroke and other types of stroke, seizures, heart arrhythmias, and death. In fact, you've undoubtedly heard about several supplement-using professional athletes who became severely ill or collapsed and died. It doesn't matter that you're a physically fit, healthy young adult or that you follow the recommended dosage on the label. Supplements can be dangerous!

> Why waste a career to build a little extra muscle mass? It's not worth it! Flat out—don't do it! Legal, illegal, it does not matter, because the consequences far outweigh the benefits. Even legal drugs, like diet supplements, are not worthy of a second glance on a store shelf. Not only can they get you in trouble, but they can cause serious bodily damage. Plain and simple, be careful and be smart in your choices.
>
> — Audra Lissell

TIME-OUT!

Confidential exercise: Make a list of the over-the-counter and prescription medications and dietary supplements you've taken over the past 4 weeks. Make an appointment with your team physician or a doctor at the campus health services to discuss the wisdom and safety of taking them.

FRIENDS DON'T NECESSARILY KNOW BEST. Teammates and friends might encourage you to try a dietary supplement that worked miracles for them. But each person reacts differently to substances. A supplement that works well and is not dangerous for a friend may be unsafe for you. Some may interfere with prescription medications you are taking or aggravate an existing medical condition.

"JUST TRY ONE; THEY'RE AMAZING." So-called friends may also encourage you to try designer or club drugs. What they're talking about are synthetic versions of various illegal drugs like heroin, amphetamines, and hallucinogens. The drugs are typically cooked up in underground labs and often used at dance parties, clubs, and bars. Common examples are MDMA (ecstasy or X), GHB, ketamine, methamphetamine (crystal meth or speed), LSD, PCP, and

Rohypnol (roofies). These are extremely dangerous. They can cause serious health problems and have even been responsible for numerous deaths. Of great concern also is that because some club drugs (like roofies) are colorless, tasteless, and odorless, they can be added to your drink without you knowing it for the purpose of intoxicating or sedating you. For example, Rohypnol is known as the date rape drug because it's used in connection with sexual assaults. So be very careful. Don't accept drinks from anyone you don't know well enough to trust; and don't leave your drink unattended, even just for a moment when you go to the rest room.

BE CAREFUL ABOUT OTHER DEPENDENCIES. Addictions don't have to be to drugs. People also can become dependent on other activities. Although you may not think of them as addictions, be careful of uncontrolled shopping and spending more money than you have, borrowing excessive amounts of money you can't pay back, signing up for high-interest credit cards and running up large bills or maxing them out, gambling in general or betting on sports events, obsessively talking on the phone, and even compulsive and inappropriate sexual activity.

THE JOY OF SEX? Sexual temptations may lead to excessive behaviors that can negatively impact sleep patterns, academic and athletic focus, and your overall health. Much has been written about the rampant spread of sexually transmitted diseases (STDs) among young adults and their potentially devastating consequences. Don't take these warnings lightly. If you are sexually active, make sure you and your partner(s) are tested for STDs every 6 months. Also, there is no guaranteed 100% effective method of birth control. For your own protection and well-being, consult with the trained staff at your school's Health Services Center.

UNACCEPTABLE BEHAVIORS. Unfortunately, abuse in relationships, sexual harassment, and acquaintance rape are far too common among college students. Remember, you are responsible for your actions. *Being a varsity athlete does not excuse inappropriate sexual behaviors, unreasonable expectations of others, or unwanted advances.* Acting as if your status on campus gives you special privileges or exempts you from having to follow the rules of acceptable social behavior is wrong and can get you into deep trouble. In fact, just being *accused* of doing something wrong can cause tremendous problems. So think before you act. And if your college has published rules about what is considered acceptable and unacceptable dating or sexual behavior, follow them religiously. A onetime, 1-minute mistake can destroy both your academic and athletic careers.

HELP AND INFORMATION ARE AVAILABLE ON CAMPUS. Become familiar with the resources your school offers regarding all of the issues just discussed. The Counseling Center, Health Services Center, and Department of Athletics have experts available to assist you. And if you have a teammate or friend who needs help, don't close your eyes to the problem. Make sure the person gets the help he or she needs.

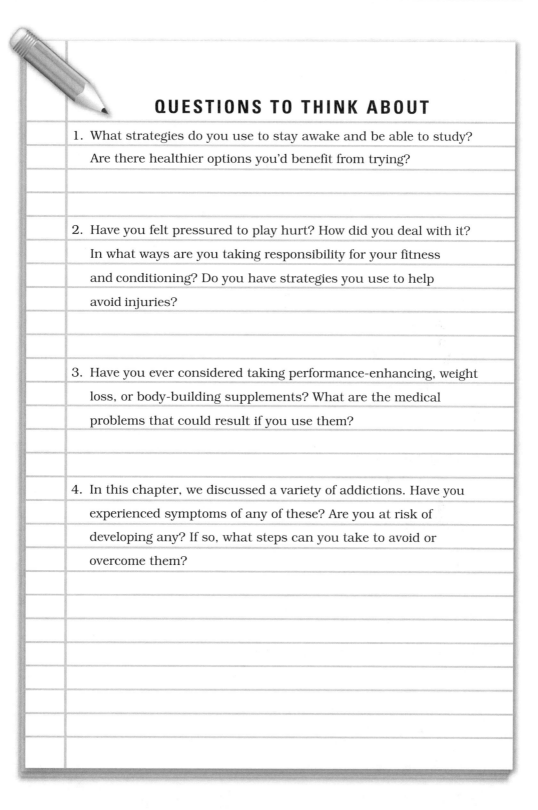

QUESTIONS TO THINK ABOUT

1. What strategies do you use to stay awake and be able to study? Are there healthier options you'd benefit from trying?

2. Have you felt pressured to play hurt? How did you deal with it? In what ways are you taking responsibility for your fitness and conditioning? Do you have strategies you use to help avoid injuries?

3. Have you ever considered taking performance-enhancing, weight loss, or body-building supplements? What are the medical problems that could result if you use them?

4. In this chapter, we discussed a variety of addictions. Have you experienced symptoms of any of these? Are you at risk of developing any? If so, what steps can you take to avoid or overcome them?

Helpful Resources

American Dietetic Association
www.eatright.org

American Social Health Association
www.ashastd.org

Centers for Disease Control and Prevention
www.cdc.gov

Harvard School of Public Health
www.hsph.harvard.edu/nutritionsource/pyramids.html

HealthierUS.Gov
www.healthierus.gov

Higher Education Center for Alcohol and Other Drug Abuse
and Violence Prevention
www.edc.org/hec

National AIDS Hotline
www.aidshotline.org
1-800-342-AIDS

National Athletic Trainers' Association
www.nata.org

National Center for Drug Free Sport
www.drugfreesport.com
816-474-8655

National Institute of Mental Health
www.nimh.nih.gov

National Institute on Drug Abuse
www.nida.nih.gov

National Women's Health Information Center
www.4woman.gov

U.S. Anti-Doping Agency (USADA)
www.usantidoping.org
Drug Reference Line: 1-800-233-0393

U.S. Department of Agriculture
www.mypyramid.gov

CHAPTER 12

Moving On

Transitions After Eligibility and College

> Upon commencement, I felt very proud of my accomplishments as a student-athlete, but at the same time, I was very nervous and uncertain about my future in the real world. I remember feeling a little bit lost. . . . I was going to have to start over in a completely new stage of my life and I was not going to have the safety net of being an athlete to help me! It was a very exciting and scary time. I felt as if everything that defined me was changing drastically.
>
> — Darci Pemberton Desilet

Commencement, simply stated, means "a beginning." And in a very real sense, commencement—the end of your undergraduate studies and, most likely, of your athletic eligibility—marks a beginning for you: the beginning of the rest of your adult life. So it's not surprising that Darci Pemberton Desilet experienced a wide range of emotions at this significant transitional event: pride, nervousness, uncertainty, fear, and excitement. These feelings aren't unique to student-athletes. They're shared by almost all college students faced with the prospect of leaving campus and moving out into the real world.

Think about it. For the last 16 years or more, you've been a student. That means you've been sheltered in a relatively safe and secure space called *school.* And as an athlete, that separate space has included an additional protected reality called *team.* But commencement or the end of eligibility brings you face to face with a new reality. No more hotel and flight bookings made for you, meals provided, teammates and coaches supporting you on a daily basis, tutors when you need them, people being extra nice just because you're an athlete, or applause from the stands. Unless you're part of that tiny 1% of college athletes who move on to the pro ranks, the world beyond playing college sports beckons, and there's no guarantee of what it will bring. The only sure thing is that the possibilities are endless.

Sooner or later, you will have to confront a range of issues related to no longer being a student-athlete. To help you face these issues, in this chapter your peers speak from a different vantage point—as graduates. Here they share their thoughts about life after eligibility and undergraduate school: about what they've done and what they hope to do; learned and hope to learn.

Whatever stage you're at in your college career (and even if it hasn't yet begun), there's much to learn from the student-athletes who contributed to this book. You and they share many of the same academic and athletic experiences, along with many of the same personal characteristics and ways of thinking. And like them, you'll have many decisions to make and options to choose from once you've earned your degree.

Tips from Peers and Profs

Commencement: A Time of Reflection

THE YEARS FLY BY. When you're facing the demands of being both a student and an athlete, some days feel like they'll never end. But before you know it, your undergraduate studies and playing days are over. Like it or not, often before you want them to, your college years come to an end and with them go the excitement, pride, friendship, and camaraderie that you wish would last forever.

> I couldn't believe four years went by so fast. It was hard to believe my time at Rutgers had come to an end and that a completely new life lay ahead. I was excited for the change but sad for leaving a place that meant so much to me.
>
> — Erin McIntyre

> Throughout my senior year, all my friends and I could talk about was "getting out of school," but now that the moment had finally arrived, we all wanted to turn around and do it all over again. Those four years were like no others in our lives: a time we will never have again nor ever forget.
>
> — Audra Lissell

EXPECT A MIX OF FEELINGS. As you probably felt at your high school graduation ceremony and at other festivities throughout senior year, college commencement is typically a time filled with joy, appreciation, high expectations, and excitement, combined with some discomfort, anxiety, and apprehension about what the future holds.

I think it was only beginning to hit me that I was ending a major phase of my life, one which had led to many positive growths and changes in me. So I mostly felt happiness to be surrounded by these people who had become my family over the past four years, but was also beginning to feel a little confusion and anxiety about what my life would be like after I left this sanctuary that Brandeis had become for me.

— Mariko Tansey Holbrook

I actually walked during the Fall 2003 commencement ceremony because our track and field conference championships was the same weekend as Spring 2003 commencement. I felt it was necessary to participate in the ceremony as a way to make my undergraduate journey final. It was overwhelming and somewhat sad to know that this part of my life was complete. And at the same time, I was very proud of my accomplishments.

— Angela Whyte

FEELINGS OF LOSS. By the time you reach commencement, you and your teammates will have spent years together in an incredibly intense way. So when it hits you that it's coming to an end, don't be surprised if you experience strong feelings of loss—of companionship, camaraderie, and friendships. Chances are you'll find yourself missing the exhilaration of competition, the locker room horsing around, and, believe it or not, even the exhausting workouts and painful training sessions with your college teammates. Those days will be over. Although that's truly sad, remember how fortunate you were to have experienced them at all. And think of the incredible opportunities and adventures that the future holds.

I miss the feeling I had when we were in the huddle down by two. Sweating, exhausted, we knew we had to go out there and leave whatever else we had in us out on the floor. I miss the competition, miss being in really tip-top shape. I miss the respect you get for being an athlete. I miss those really, really hard practices when you just wanted to quit right then and there, but when you were done you felt amazing that you just accomplished that. I miss basketball so much!

— Johanna DiChiara-Drab

> I miss the camaraderie and the adrenaline that comes with soccer. It's depressing to think about. In perfect shape, running full speed to knock someone off the ball and pass it or shoot. The crowd cheering. The attention. The satisfaction of making a good play. The trust in my teammates. As a sport that I've played competitively every day for 15 years, there is a huge hole that is left when it stops.
>
> — David Ledet

TIME-OUT!

Describe three things you'll miss when your varsity days are over. What feelings do you think will accompany those losses?

THE REAL WORLD BECKONS. There's no avoiding it. Sooner or later, all students have to move on to life beyond college—life as an independent adult, a life that is demanding in new and different ways—and into a world filled with uncertainties, unknowns, and unlimited possibilities for personal growth and fulfillment.

> I was now entering the real world. For most of us, collegiate athletics shields you in a way. It creates this world where all you do is play a sport and go to class. I thought about no longer being part of this world and being forced to perform, whether it is academically or professionally, in a different way.
>
> — Jason Roberts

> One of the most difficult periods of postgraduation was the realization that I was now on my own. There was no longer the safety net of professors, coaches, or college. Success or failure was solely due to my actions. Added to this pressure was the stress of wondering if I was doing "what I was supposed to do" in terms of my career and professional aspirations.
>
> — Douglas White

> At graduation, I can remember feeling overwhelmed with leaving all of the great friends I had met, job hunting, and becoming an independent, bill-paying adult. I feel so grown up now. It feels very adult to be paying a mortgage and going food shopping and doing all those other grown-up things that become routine.
>
> — Patricia Metzger

What Does the Future Hold?

THE BIGGEST CONCERN. Sooner or later, every college student has to face the same question: What am I going to do after I graduate? Some begin thinking about it as early as elementary school; others while they're in high school. Still others manage (or seem to manage) to avoid giving thought to it until the last semester of their senior year. Although it's a good idea to start thinking about your future as early as possible, no matter when you begin thinking about what you're going to do after graduation, the months right before commencement can be a most anxious time. After all, the only thing you can be absolutely sure about is that your life is going to change dramatically. The possibilities are endless.

RIGHT AFTER COLLEGE. Many of our contributors went to graduate or professional school in education, exercise science, finance, law, marketing, mechanical engineering, philosophy, medicine, public health, sport psychology, and theology. Two became teachers. Some went pro or continued to compete at a high level: beach volleyball in California, football with the Dallas Cowboys, basketball in Europe. One trained for and competed in the 2004 Olympics, finishing sixth in the final of the women's 100-meter hurdles. Others became assistant coaches at the college level. A number found employment: as a physical therapist in Philadelphia, an auditor in New York City, a model in Chicago, a consumer sales representative in Atlanta, and a credit relationship manager in Brooklyn, New York (after completing a 6-month internship while still in college). One received a prestigious fellowship to study in India, another traveled through Europe, and still another through the western United States, tent camping and visiting national parks. And finally, just 6 days after commencement, one of our contributors began working for the California governor's office. Less than 6 months later, after the governor lost a recall election, our student-athlete found himself "down, but not out." He soon "landed on his feet" as a legislative assistant with the NCAA's Office of Government Relations.

TWO YEARS LATER. Several have gotten married, and one is on maternity leave from teaching fifth grade—she reports having a boy who at 2 weeks old was already shooting jump shots! Two followed their entrepreneurial instincts, and one temporarily withdrew from graduate school to become owner/operator of a family entertainment center. Another, after completing his graduate degree in finance, became a partner in a tennis academy where he is able to merge his education with his love of the sport. A number have moved into public service positions, one as a Peace Corps volunteer in China working alongside her husband, and another as the coordinator of a marine science environmental organization. Many have continued with their careers in accounting, coaching, commercial banking, physical therapy, sales, and teaching—some with the same employers and others with different employers and in new cities.

SOME CHOSE TO MOVE ON; OTHERS HAD TO. For example, the NCAA legislative assistant has become part of the management team for an industrial supply company, has begun work on a master's degree in public administration, and hopes eventually to run for political office. Unfortunately, our professional beach volleyball player tore up her knee. She now freelances as a high-tech consultant while applying to graduate programs. The pro basketball player has returned from stints in Italy, Spain, and France and is a partner with a diversified financial services company in Maryland. And our student-athlete defensive back is still making tackles and running back kicks for the Dallas Cowboys. Although it's not always exactly what you envision, it's clear that there certainly is life after college!

TIME-OUT!

After commencement, what do you hope your *real world* will look like? What are you doing to make those hopes come true?

New Opportunities

ENJOYING NEWFOUND TIME AND FREEDOM. No longer feeling the pressure of academic and athletic obligations, many former student-athletes appreciate the time they now have to relax.

> I finally have the time to do some things I haven't been able to do before. I can play golf on the weekends. I'm going to have my first spring break since eighth grade! All the sacrifices I've made over the years—I don't have to make those sacrifices in the same way anymore. It's time to pay attention to many of the other things in life beyond baseball: family, friends, and good times.
>
> — Jim Olds

> I have freedom and more independence for the big things, the freedom to travel more and not being tied down to so many commitments with athletics and classes.
>
> — Julie Ruff

> I look forward to watching my son grow up, furthering my education, and to my life with my husband. I chose this as opposed to playing basketball. I know in the long run this is what is more important to me, and I can always go to the park and beat up on the boys in a pickup game!
>
> — Johanna DiChiara-Drab

PURSUING NEW ATHLETIC CHALLENGES. By the time they graduate, some college athletes have spent so many years training and competing in one sport, they feel somewhat burned out. Many had a long-standing interest in trying other sports—both recreationally and competitively—but during their varsity careers they weren't able to find the time or make the necessary commitment. After graduation, they do. Swimmers take up running, runners pursue cycling, and many play golf.

> Since I have retired from swimming, I am enjoying the free time I have to explore other sports such as running, biking, hiking, rowing, and snowboarding.
>
> — Katie Younglove

> I've chosen to pursue other sports such as cycling. It has renewed my excitement for training and competing while exposing me to a variety of new people. Although running and cycling are very different, the training methodologies and systems are strikingly similar. Thus running prepared me for cycling not only in general fitness and endurance but also in training techniques and mind-sets.
>
> — Seth Neumuller

A DESIRE TO BENEFIT OTHERS. With their time freed up and energy renewed, many recently graduated college athletes look to extend themselves by helping others in an effort to give back to their communities.

> I am now on a different journey. I can't tell you when was the last time I picked up a basketball. My life is focused on God, family, and creativity. I am looking forward to becoming a more thoughtful person, and I am also going to be a multimillionaire. I have to. I need to be able to help people outside of my family. When I see the homeless, disabled, or unfortunate, it tears my heart apart. I need to make a difference in that area.
>
> — Maurice Yearwood

> Another goal I devoted myself to was to give back to the community as much as possible. I have already done food drives, visited the Children's Hospital of Dallas, spoke at various schools, and done charitable work with the victims of Hurricane Katrina. As my career grows as a player (National Football League) and businessman, I hope to start my own charitable foundation for cancer, AIDS, or some other social problem that people are dealing with today.
>
> — Nate Jones

> I am looking forward to starting a career and hopefully being able to help other people make physical activity an enduring, healthy aspect of their lives—and years from now transitioning into a teaching and coaching role for new runners.
>
> — Mariko Tansey Holbrook

FURTHER EDUCATION. Many student-athletes continue on to graduate or professional schools immediately after graduation, but others put it off for a while. After a year or two away from life as a student, though, they return to the classroom to further their education. Although paying for it can be a serious concern, many are able to secure fellowships or graduate assistantships, are sponsored by their employers, or work as college assistant coaches or dorm resident advisors in exchange for tuition remission and/or free on-campus housing.

> I'm looking forward to returning to school for a master's degree and experiencing the college life once again, enjoying the company of friends, and receiving even more education. I realize what I could have changed in college, how I could have made it a better experience—and I want to replace my regrets with opportunity. Not everyone gets a second chance, but I hope to.
>
> — Audra Lissell

TEAM BONDS LIVE ON. Many athletes speak about how they think of their college team as a second family. And the closeness they feel to their teammates, coaches, and school doesn't end with graduation. Keeping up with how their old college team is doing is important to them. They stay in touch with former teammates and coaches, return to campus, attend competitions at home and on the road, and provide encouragement to still active former teammates as well as new members of the team. You may find yourself doing much of the same.

> Coach Flannery and Coach Friday and I speak about once a month, catching up on old times and new. I look forward to making it back to games. I will be flying down to the Duke game to support the squad as they take on the Blue Devils.
>
> — Dan Blankenship

> I look forward to going back to Rutgers for meets and Homecoming to support the team that meant so much to me.
>
> — Erin McIntyre

CONFRONTING NEW CHALLENGES. You didn't become a varsity athlete by shying away from challenges. You confronted them head on and made the most of whatever new situations came your way. Commencement means you're faced with a set of new challenges. And no one can be sure of exactly what they will be. That may be cause for some anxiety, but just as in your athletic endeavors, those challenges are also opportunities to shine.

> There is a lot to look forward to. My undergraduate education prepared me with a variety of options in choosing a profession, and it also equipped me with the ability to continue excelling. I don't yet know exactly what I'll be doing, but I know I'll try hard to be the best. That might be the thing I'm looking forward to the most—the challenge.
>
> — David Ledet

> Don't be afraid to try new things. Life is about new experiences and you can't grow as a person if you always stay with what you know.
>
> — Douglas White

Refining Abilities and Strengths

THOSE POSITIVE ATTRIBUTES AGAIN. In chapter 1, you were asked to think seriously about a range of personal attributes that are extremely valuable. Undoubtedly, you possess many of these qualities. Among them are discipline, adaptability, a strong work ethic, commitment, perseverance, and self-confidence. Our contributors possessed these when they began college as well. After graduating, they reflected on the personal characteristics and traits, abilities, and strengths that are transferable to life after undergraduate school. What they reported, not surprisingly, is that the same attributes that enabled them to succeed academically and athletically in college remain the keys to success in the real world. So consider again which of these attributes you already possess, which you need to work on, and how you can best use them to one day make a successful transition to work, graduate or professional school, and family and community life.

Discipline

College shaped my character in countless ways that impact my life today. Being a student-athlete taught me balance, discipline, perseverance, and independence. For example, being an athlete taught me discipline in my eating, sleeping, studying, and social habits. Those skills that I developed as a swimmer have proved valuable in my life as a graduate student and employee.

— Katie Younglove

Adaptability

I have confidence that I can adapt to any situation. For instance, if I find a job not completely related to my degree, I will be able to adapt. I have confidence that I can excel in most anything that I put my mind to.

— Angela Whyte

Rutgers was an *enormous* school that required a lot of maneuvering for a new student. It was an environment that promoted the mentality of sink or swim. So I swam, and swam hard. I had to adapt in order to cope and ultimately survive the hurdles and stresses that I encountered. If I had not mastered this skill, I would not have made it there, in graduate school, or even in my workplace.

— Courtney Turner

Work Ethic

Playing college basketball forces you to work hard. If you don't work harder than the next guy, you will fail. The hard work and determination that I needed to be successful in basketball and school have done wonders for my career. In sales, people never want to listen to what you have to say. Rarely do people return phone calls or e-mails I send them. Because of my ability to be persistent and work hard, I'm able to get business when other people would have just given up.

— Jon Larranaga

When I was job hunting, the fact that I was an athlete was an added advantage. Many of my interviews were with a former student-athlete (or someone who had a child who was an athlete), and as a result of the reputation/perception of an athlete's work ethic, I received many job offers (literally).

— Courtney Turner

Commitment

I learned how to stay committed to something. There were many people I knew who did not finish playing sports in college or did not earn their degree. I learned how to commit to something and plan so that I could accomplish the goal and finish what I started. I use this in daily life. If I make a commitment to something, I am going to do what it takes to get it done.

— Brandi Cross

Commitment is definitely helping me through the trials of living in China right now, and also the commitment to myself to do what I think is best for me and my loved ones' lives.

— Anna (Doty) Ramirez

Perseverance

Perseverance to me is being able to hang in there through the darkest hour— being able to push through it, whatever it is. Not many people can do that. In life there are going to be really hard times: basketball, school, friends, career, relationships, etc. The hardest thing to do is to just stick with it. I feel sports and college gave me this, and I treasure it more than all the things I learned in my college career.

— Johanna DiChiara Drab

I worked my way from a freshman walk-on to a full scholarship athlete because I chose to persevere through four years of athletics. Even with three shoulder surgeries and one knee surgery, I still never regret my choice to press on through the relentless rehab process and get back to optimal condition. Perseverance still gets me through my long days at the hospital and even longer nights buried in my medical textbooks. I know what I have to do to get where I want to be, and I will persevere through all obstacles to get there.

— Ashley Ready

Self-confidence

I learned that I can do anything I set my mind to. Completing a college degree humbled me but built my confidence that I am capable and strong and meant to have a place in this world.

— Jenifer Martin-Flake

I entered as a young, immature basketball player and left an academic, with the ability to perform under any circumstances—being an athlete at a top-notch academic institution prepares you for almost anything. You hardly have time to do anything, but being able to succeed despite this is something you carry for the rest of your life.

— Jason Roberts

Lessons Learned

DEVELOPING NEW SKILLS, ABILITIES, AND ATTRIBUTES. The student-athletes we spoke with also appreciate the new skills, abilities, and attributes their college academic and athletic pursuits provided or, in some cases, required them to develop. And all of these have tremendous value in the real world.

Time Management

Time management is the best skill I learned in college. Having to juggle practice, game tape, conditioning, and a full-time course load, I quickly learned how to prioritize and plan what to do and when. As a teacher, this helps me fulfill both my inside-the-classroom and outside-the-classroom duties without feeling so stressed.

— Brandi Cross

Balance

My experience at Mason helped me achieve the "life skills" I have needed to be successful. I learned so much more than was taught in the textbooks and lectures—time management, balance, and patience. Being able to balance schoolwork with basketball and volleyball, as well as have time for myself, was difficult in college. I find that managing time has helped me find ways to be efficient with work, school, working out, friends, family, and so on.

— Shelbylynn McBride

Patience

There was a lot of stress in my life during those 4 years, and it was all on campus. After my first 2 years, I realized everything happens for a reason. You have to be patient and let life take her course. Also, never stress over things you have no control over.

— Maurice Yearwood

Respect for Diversity

I met so many people from so many walks of the earth. It wasn't until attending LIU that I realized how sheltered I had been. I grew up attending Catholic school and surrounded myself with Irish Catholics in all aspects of my life. Then I moved to Brooklyn and realized that there is *soooo* much more out there. This has really helped me with interacting with and being sensitive to the needs of my patients.

— Patricia Metzger

I learned how to work with others, and learned a lot about different cultures and just differences between people. I also learned a lot about human relationships, which helps me daily through any activity.

— Anna (Doty) Ramirez

Compromise

I learned to compromise. With 20 girls on a team, you must realize that you cannot always have your way. There has to be a middle road.

— Patricia Metzger

Communication

From small social situations, to large-scale presentations, to office meetings with faculty and coaches, I learned how to share my thoughts appropriately. I never had a problem talking to people, but college opened me up and gave me the opportunity to share myself with others from a verbal standpoint.

— Audra Lissell

Assertiveness

No one in life is going to do anything for you except you. This mentality has helped me oh so much! If I actually sat back and waited for someone to make the decisions and get the job done for me, I would probably still have the credits of a freshman.

— Courtney Turner

Critical Thinking Skills

I learned how to think critically, which is one of the most valuable skills one can develop. A college graduate is nothing without a heightened ability to think critically and problem-solve.

— Jenifer Martin-Flake

Mental Toughness

As an athlete, I experienced so many times when my life was really difficult. My body was hurt on several occasions and I had to rehabilitate through pain; we had extremely hard physical/mental practices and I had to learn how to push through; we lost games and I had to learn to forget, get better, and move on; and I had to sacrifice a lot of the fun of ordinary college life for my sport. All of my experiences with hardship have helped me deal with new situations that arise in my life.

— Darci Pemberton Desilet

Independence

Learning to fend for myself and be independent is one of the most useful abilities I gained in college, and thankfully so as I move on in my career. College forces you to grow up quickly. Those who are able to make that transition will have a better chance of success than those who still rely on others to take care of them or help them out with every little thing.

— Audra Lissell

Perspective

I was constantly comparing myself to others and striving to be the best. I realize now that my life lacked balance in college, especially in my early years. I focused on swimming and my studies so much that I missed out on other opportunities. Through my successes and failures, I learned to see a bigger picture. I regret that I did not take advantage of all the cultural and social opportunities around me. Today, I still try to do my best, but I am more able to discern which things are truly important. My mistakes in the past have helped me become a more balanced person today.

— Katie Younglove

It is so easy to get caught up with the little things that happen to you. My experience helped me to look beyond some of the trivial things in my life and spend my precious time on what is important—my friends and family. I learned to look a little more at the big picture of things.

— Darci Pemberton Desilet

The value of our college experience does not rest in that final day, but instead on the steps we took to get there. What we learn in a college setting only gives us a basis for whatever it is we may do once we leave school—it is what sparks our interest and makes us realize that the majority of the learning we have to do is still ahead of us.

— Jim Olds

Closing Notes

HERE'S TO YOU! We hope the time you've spent with this book has been productive and you've learned valuable lessons from the authors (the profs) and just as importantly from your peers. They have gone well beyond surviving—to thriving as students, athletes, and contributing members of their communities. If you have gained only one thing from what you've read, we hope it's this: *No one can control the future, but you can be prepared for it.* We sincerely hope we've helped in your preparation so that you, too, can thrive in college as well as beyond. We wish you the best in everything you do.

WE'D LIKE YOUR INPUT. We wrote this book with you in mind. And your ideas, reactions, and suggestions are important to us. So please take a few minutes and let us know what you think. What have you found particularly useful?

What changes would you recommend? And what questions do you still have that you'd like answered? The best way to contact us is via email at robert.nathanson@liu.edu or arthur.kimmel@liu.edu. Thank you for your help.

FINAL QUESTION TO THINK ABOUT

On graduation day, will you be able to say, "I really got the most from my college experience"? What are you doing to make sure you'll be able to say it?

Profiles of Featured Student-Athletes

A. DAVID ALSTON

A graduate of Kent State University with a degree in justice studies, David was a 4-year starting running back on the football team and an All Mid-American Conference (MAC) running back in his sophomore year. Inducted into the National Criminal Justice Honor Society and twice named All MAC Academic Running Back of the Year, as a junior he was one of only 200 student-athletes chosen (from over 5,000 applicants) to attend the NCAA Foundation Leadership Conference in Orlando, Florida.

DAN BLANKENSHIP

Dan graduated from Bucknell University with a degree in accounting. A Dean's List student, he was twice named Patriot League Scholar Athlete of the Year. Dan was co-captain of the men's basketball team for 2 years, directing play from his position as point guard and earning team awards for leadership, spirit, intensity, and excellence in defense. After graduation, he began working as an analyst for a major financial services corporation.

DAN BRADLEY

Dan is a summa cum laude graduate of Bradley University with a degree in philosophy. He was named Philosophy Student of the Year, captained the golf team, and was selected to attend the NCAA Foundation Leadership Conference. After graduation Dan continued his education, earning an MA in philosophy from the University of South Carolina. He then went on to become owner of a family entertainment facility.

BRANDI CROSS

A summa cum laude graduate of the University of Massachusetts–Amherst, with a degree in psychology, Brandi was a standout at first base for the softball team. She was the first-ever Verizon Academic All-American Team Member of the Year from UMass, was named Atlantic-10 Student Athlete of the Year, and was selected as the UMass Female Scholar Athlete of the Year and twice Atlantic-10 All-Conference First Baseman. She continued her education at Boston College, earning a master's degree in elementary education, and is an elementary school teacher.

DARCI PEMBERTON DESILET

Recipient of the Rich and Mary Fox Scholarship for the student-athlete at the University of Idaho with the highest overall GPA as a senior, Darci graduated with a degree in physical education and double minor in health and psychology. She played small forward on the UI women's basketball team, was selected for the Verizon Academic All-District VIII first and second team, first team Academic All-Big West, and was twice named second team All-Big West. A physical education teacher, Darci expects to pursue a graduate degree in education.

JOHANNA DICHIARA-DRAB

Johanna began her higher education at Dowling College and graduated from Long Island University–Brooklyn Campus, with a degree in elementary education. A Dean's List student, she played center on the women's basketball team. At Dowling, Johanna earned All-American Honorable Mention honors, and one season ranked third in the nation in blocked shots. She is a elementary school teacher whose goal is to attain a PhD in history.

TIM DONNELLY

A magna cum laude graduate of California State–Fullerton, Tim maintained a perfect 4.0 GPA in his major, kinesiology. A midfielder for the Titans and captain his senior year, he was named Big West Conference Men's Soccer Team Scholar-Athlete of the Year, Big West Scholar-Athlete of the Year, and was a California State–Fullerton Student Leader Recognition Award recipient. Tim works as a marketing representative for Nike.

LAUREN FENDRICK

Lauren, a communication studies (mass media) major, graduated from UCLA magna cum laude. A 4-year volleyball outside hitter and 1-year softball pitcher/pinch hitter, she earned First Team Verizon Academic All-American and ac-10 Academic All-American honors. Lauren was the sixth Bruin to record over 1,000 kills, 1,000 digs, and 100 aces in UCLA women's volleyball history.

JILL FIRMAN

During her 3 years as an undergraduate at the University of Cincinnati (before beginning a pharmacy doctoral program), Jill maintained an exemplary GPA. She was a center mid-fielder and outside defender on the women's soccer team, and she twice was named to the Conference USA Commissioner's Honor Roll and to the Bobcat Honor Roll four times.

ABRAHAM BILLY HARDEE III

Abraham attended Florida Southern College, where he was a defensive wing on the soccer team, and he graduated from Virginia Tech with a major in the science of food nutrition and exercise. A Dean's List student at Tech and Big East Academic A Team member, he played football (strong safety, cornerback, and free safety), earning the Top Defensive Hustler Award, and was a center fielder on the baseball team. After graduation, Abraham began medical school at the Virginia College of Osteopathic Medicine, in pursuit of his goal of becoming a missionary doctor.

SPENCER HARRIS

A Dean's List student for 4 years, second team Academic All-American, and Virginia Tech Scholar Athlete of the Year, Spencer majored in nutrition. Captain of the baseball team his senior year, he was named First Team All-Big East and held the Virginia Tech record for most games started in a career and most assists, most putouts, and most double plays by a shortstop. Spencer hopes to open a family practice medical clinic after completing his studies at the Virginia College of Osteopathic Medicine.

MARIKO TANSEY HOLBROOK

Junior year Phi Beta Kappa inductee and magna cum laude graduate of Brandeis University, Mariko majored in biology. A cross-country and indoor and outdoor track standout in the 1,500, 3,000, and 5,000 meters, she is a three-time NCAA Division III Cross-Country, three-time NCAA Division III Indoor Track, and three-time NCAA Division III Outdoor Track All-American. After graduation, Mariko continued her education at Northeastern University, working toward an MS in physician assistant studies with the goal of becoming a physician's assistant and physical activity advocate.

BECKY HUNNEWELL

Majoring in elementary education and French and Francophone studies, Becky graduated from the University of Massachusetts–Amherst. A two-season captain of the swim team, she was named to the Atlantic 10 All-Conference Academic Team and the Commissioner's Honor Roll. Twice A-10 Champion in the 100- and 200-yard backstroke, and once in the 100-yard freestyle, Becky was a Dean's List student and was named A-10 Most Valuable Player 2 years in a row. After graduation, she began teaching fourth grade while pursuing a master's degree in elementary education.

JENNIFER JOHNSTONE

A Dean's List student, Jennifer graduated from the University of Maine–Orono as a secondary education major with a concentration in mathematics. Playing center midfield on the field hockey team, she was a First Team Regional All-American and two-time First Team All-Conference selection. Jennifer also received the Dean Smith Award for outstanding athletic, academic, and community service and the Presidential Academic Achievement Award. After graduation, she continued to be involved with field hockey, serving as assistant coach at Brown University.

NATE JONES

A two-time Academic All-American, three-time member of the Big East All Academic Team, and National Football Foundation Scholar Athlete of the Year as a senior, Nate majored in finance at Rutgers University, graduating with high honors. Although his main sport was football (cornerback and kickoff returner), he was also a member of the track team (sprint and long jump). After graduation, Nate began a career in professional football, playing for the Dallas Cowboys.

JON LARRANAGA

A communications major and Dean's List student, Jon graduated from George Mason University. He played forward on the basketball team and was twice named to both the Colonial Athletic Association All-Defensive Team and All-Academic Team. In addition, Jon was named to the Division I-AAA Athletic Director's Association Scholar-Athlete Team. After graduation, he played for Ireland's national basketball team and then became a partner in sales for a major financial services corporation.

DAVID LEDET

Class valedictorian and summa cum laude graduate of Long Island University–Brooklyn Campus, David had a double major: political science and English. A defender and midfielder on the soccer team, he was named to the ESPN Academic All-American first Team. David was also a member of the University Honors Program, a Jeannette K. Watson Fellow, and a Center for the Study of the Presidency Fellow. After graduation, he accepted a summer internship with the M.V. Foundation in Hyderabad, India, and prepared a report detailing and analyzing the benefits of education for former child laborers in rural Andhra Pradesh, India.

AUDRA LISSELL

A Dean's List student and inductee into the National Society of College Scholars, Audra graduated from Brandeis University with a major in American Studies. She was a 2-year All-Academic University Athletic Association team member and 2-year starting forward on the Judges basketball team, leading the team in rebounding and blocked shots and the league in 3-point field goal percentage. Off the court she wrote for the *The Justice* (the university's newspaper) and served as yearbook sports editor. After graduation, Audra began working for the New England Aquarium as coordinator/administrative assistant of the Marine Conservation Action Fund.

JENIFER MARTIN-FLAKE

Multiple Dean's List honoree and onetime Scholar-Athlete of the Year, Jenifer graduated with honors from California State University–Fullerton, having majored in child and adolescent development. A cross-country and track standout in the 10,000 and 5,000 meters, as well as the 2- and 1-mile distances, she earned the Best Performance of the Year Award in 2001–2002. After graduation, Jenifer continued her education and received a master's of education and CLAD Certificate from Azusa Pacific. She then became a sixth-grade language arts/social science teacher, leadership advisor, and head cross-country coach at a public school. Jenifer has also begun work on a doctorate in education.

SHELBYLYNN MCBRIDE

Shelbylynn graduated cum laude from George Mason University having majored in sociology. A Dean's List and Athletic Director's Honor Roll student, this two-sport athlete played basketball (guard) for 4 years and volleyball (opposite side) for 3. She was named Colonial Athletic Association Rookie of the Year and twice a CAA Scholar-Athlete. After graduation, Shelbylynn became assistant volleyball coach/recruiting coordinator at Towson University.

ERIN MCINTYRE

A standout performer in the classroom and in the pool (specializing in the 500- and 1,650-yard freestyle and 400-yard individual medley), Erin majored in mechanical engineering and graduated from Rutgers University with highest honors. On top of making Dean's List every semester and being recognized at the national convention of Tau Beta Pi (the national engineering honors society) for excellence in academics and athletics, she earned the Rutgers President's Award for achieving a perfect 4.0 GPA one semester. Erin was also a three-time Division I All-American and was named the Big East Conference Female Student-Athlete of the Year. After graduation she began working on a master's degree in mechanical engineering at the University of Michigan.

PATRICIA METZGER

A multiple Dean's List honoree, Patricia graduated cum laude from Long Island University–Brooklyn Campus with a BS/MS in physical therapy. This two-sport athlete (soccer, defender; track, 500 meters, 4 × 400 relay, 400 individual hurdles, and 400-meter dash) was a two-time Northeast Conference 500-meter champion in track and was named second team All-Conference Defender in soccer. Upon graduation, Patricia became a senior physical therapist at Frankford Hospital Outpatient Physical Therapy Center and began studying toward her doctorate of physical therapy at Widener University.

SETH NEUMULLER

Seth began his undergraduate education at UCLA where he maintained an exemplary GPA while competing in cross country and track. He graduated magna cum laude from Rice University (where he also ran cross country and track) with a BS in chemical engineering. As a senior, Seth was inducted into Phi Beta Kappa and received the Ann and Joe Hightower Superior Award in chemical engineering for graduating at the top of his class. In addition, he was winner of the Hubert E. Bray Male Scholar-Athlete of the Year Award in 2005. Upon graduation, Seth worked as a production engineer for a major chemical company in Texas.

JIM OLDS

A summa cum laude graduate of the University of Cincinnati, Jim received a bachelor's in business administration, with a concentration in finance. A four-letter athlete, playing catcher, pitcher, and outfielder on the baseball team, he made Dean's List every quarter, was awarded the Conference USA Commissioner's Medal for Academic Excellence each year of his eligibility, and was named Top Cat Scholar Athlete of the Year as a senior. After graduating, Jim began studying law at Indiana University School of Law–Bloomington, with an eye toward working in athletic administration at the college level.

ROYCE RAMEY

Royce majored in finance at Texas Tech University and graduated summa cum laude, earning President's List and Dean's List honors. For 2 years he led the tennis team playing the number-one singles position and was named first team All Big 12, first team Academic All Big 12, and Texas Tech Student-Athlete of the Year. After graduation, Royce earned a master of science in finance and became a partner in a tennis academy. He then changed careers and joined a full-service wealth management firm in Phoenix, Arizona.

ANNA (DOTY) RAMIREZ

Four times named Scholar-Athlete, including Female Track & Field Athlete of the Year as a junior, Anna graduated from California State University–Fullerton with a BS in kinesiology. A triple jump and long jump specialist, she was named All-Conference five times and held school records for the triple jump, long jump, and heptathlon. After graduating, she earned her teaching credential in physical education and a supplementary in health at CSU–Fullerton, then joined the Peace Corps and served as a volunteer, teaching oral English and American culture/history to English majors at Yibin University in China.

ASHLEY READY

Ashley was a magna cum laude graduate of Texas Tech University as a psychology major. She was on the Dean's List every semester, and one semester she made the President's List with a perfect 4.0. A catcher on the softball team, she began her varsity career as a walk-on, but by her senior year she was awarded an academic-athletic scholarship, was nominated as team captain, and had earned first team All Big 12 Conference Academic Honors. After graduation, Ashley entered a graduate program in physician assistant studies at the University of Texas Medical Branch at Galveston and became co-director at St. Vincent's Clinic (a nonprofit indigent health-care clinic managed and staffed by volunteer medical and physician assistant students).

JASON K. ROBERTS

A two-time Dean's List student while playing forward and center on the Judges basketball team, Jason graduated from Brandeis University. He majored in American Studies with a program in Legal Studies and served as an intern with the East Boston District Court. Indicative of his basketball prowess, Jason was twice named University Athletic Association Player of the Week. After graduation, he continued working toward his goal of becoming an attorney by enrolling at the George Washington University Law School.

JULIE RUFF

Julie graduated summa cum laude as a marketing major from Kent State University, where she was a middle blocker and captain of the volleyball team. A Verizon Academic All-American and member of the Academic All-MAC Team, she was named to the Dean's List seven semesters and represented Kent State at the NCAA Leadership Conference. After graduation, Julie became a youth director and head youth pastor while studying at Fuller Theological Seminary for master's degrees in marriage and family therapy and in divinity.

COURTNEY TURNER

Courtney earned her bachelor's degree in public health while a vault and floor specialist on the gymnastics team at Rutgers University. A multiyear NCAA Academic All-American and Dean's List honoree, she earned Female Athlete of the Year honors and was Rutgers' first-ever NCAA Division 1 National Qualifier. Following graduation, Courtney studied at Emory University, earning a master's of public health, and she took a position with the U.S. Department of Health and Human Services.

JILL TURNER

Earning both bachelor's and master's degrees in marketing management at Virginia Tech, Jill graduated first in her class from the Pamplin College of Business. A 2-year captain of the swim team, she specialized in the sprint freestyle and backstroke and was the school record holder in six events. While an undergraduate, Jill made the Dean's List all eight semesters, and she earned numerous awards, including Atlantic-10 Rookie of the Year, Virginia Tech Scholar Athlete of the Year, and Big East Scholar Athlete Award.

DOUG WHITE

Doug graduated magna cum laude from the University of Massachusetts as a management major. A placekicker and punter on the football team, he was the all-time UMass leader in career field-goal percentage (.771) and ranked second in career extra points made (97). Doug was a UMass Scholar-Athlete of the Year, a Verizon Academic All-American, and was named to both the Atlantic-10 Academic All-Conference and Football All-Conference teams. Following graduation, while employed on the management team of an industrial supply company, Doug pursued a master's degree in public administration at New York University.

ANGELA WHYTE

Majoring in crime and justice studies, Angela graduated from the University of Idaho, where she earned Dean's List honors, was an Arthur Ashe Sports Scholar, and the Idaho state NCAA Woman of the Year as a scholar-athlete. A four-time NCAA All-American as a hurdler, sprinter, and long jumper, Angela held 13 school records and was a two-time Big West Conference Female Track and Field Athlete of the Year. As a member of the Canadian National Team, she was a 2004 Olympic finalist in the 100-meter hurdles.

MAURICE YEARWOOD

Maurice earned both his bachelor's (double major in marketing and management) and MBA (finance) degrees at Long Island University–Brooklyn Campus while co-captaining the Blackbirds basketball team for 2 years and handling the roles of both point and shooting guard. He was an Academic All-American and an Arthur Ashe Award recipient two consecutive years, as well as an inductee into *Who's Who in American Colleges and Universities.* A successful undergraduate internship resulted in Maurice's landing a position with Citibank.

KATIE YOUNGLOVE

Katie graduated summa cum laude from UCLA as a communication studies major. A two-year Academic All-American and three-year All-American as a swimmer, she had the second fastest times in UCLA history in the 100- and 200-yard butterfly. Following graduation, Katie entered a master's degree program in theology.

About the Authors

Bob Nathanson
Long Island University–Brooklyn Campus

Dr. Bob Nathanson is associate professor of Teaching and Learning at Long Island University–Brooklyn Campus, where he has also taught in the Departments of Physical Therapy and Psychology since 1976. He has taught and advised hundreds of student-athletes during his tenure and has also taught freshman orientation seminar and summer precollege orientation courses for over 20 years. In 1993, Professor Nathanson was awarded the David Newton Award for Excellence in Teaching, the university's highest teaching honor. He has served on the university's Intercollegiate Athletics Council (IAC) since its inception in 1996. The IAC reviews virtually all aspects of the athletics program with special regard for student-athlete welfare. As a result of such careful oversight, in 2001 LIU was honored as one of nine schools to receive the inaugural USA Today/NCAA Foundation Academic Achievement Award for excellence among student-athletes. LIU was selected for having the highest student-athlete graduation rate above the average of the general student body among Division I institutions from 1994 to 2000. In 2002, LIU was a repeat winner. On May 4, 2005, Professor Nathanson was one of two faculty members honored by the LIU Department of Athletics in recognition of his "tremendous support and dedication to our student-athletes and Long Island University Athletics." Professor Nathanson is President of the Institute for Academic Success of College Athletes (IASCA), a newly formed not-for-profit corporation whose mission is to enhance the student side of the student-athlete role. Dr. Nathanson is also a member of the National Association of Academic Advisors for Athletics.

Arthur Kimmel

Long Island University–Brooklyn Campus and St. Francis College

 An adjunct professor of sociology and social work at Long Island University–Brooklyn Campus and an adjunct professor in the Sociology and Criminal Justice Department at Saint Francis College in Brooklyn, New York, Arthur Kimmel has taught and mentored hundreds of student-athletes. His research and teaching interests include the sociology of sports, popular culture, mass communications, and diversity. He is a member of the National Association of Academic Advisors for Athletics and in 2004, along with Professors Bob Nathanson and Jeff Lambert, Professor Kimmel founded the Institute for Academic Success of College Athletes, a non-profit organization created to identify, develop, and implement strategies to enhance the academic performance of college athletes.

In addition to over two decades of teaching at the university level, Professor Kimmel spent 12 years working in the advertising industry as a copywriter, copy supervisor, and associate creative director at major agencies including NW Ayer and Ogilvy & Mather Direct.

A lifelong sports fan and participant, Kimmel has coached youth and high school basketball for more than 12 years and has coached and refereed soccer for over 15 years. In addition, he holds a fourth-degree black belt in tae kwon do. Martial arts students he has taught, trained, and coached have won dozens of tournament championships in both forms and free fighting at prestigious competitions. Kimmel himself is a trophy-winning competitor and remains active on the tournament scene as a respected judge and referee.

Index